D1491279

The Agile Manager's Guide To

WRITING
TO GET ACTION

By Dennis Chambers

Velocity Business Publishing
Bristol, Vermont USA

Copyright © 1998 by Dennis Chambers
All Rights Reserved
Printed in the United States of America
Library of Congress Catalog Card Number 97-81355
ISBN 1-58099-008-8
Title page illustration by Elayne Sears

If you'd like additional copies of this book or a catalog of books in the Agile Manager Series™, please get in touch with us.

- **Write us at:**
  Velocity Business Publishing, Inc.
  15 Main Street
  Bristol, VT 05443 USA

- **Call us at:**
  1-888-805-8600 in North America (toll-free)
  1-802-453-6669 from all other countries

- **Fax us at:**
  1-802-453-2164

- **E-mail us at:**
  info@agilemanager.com

- **Visit our Web site at:**
  www.agilemanager.com

The Web site contains much of interest to business people—tips and techniques, business news, links to valuable sites, and electronic versions of titles in the Agile Manager Series.

Call or write for a free, time-saving "extra-fast" edition of this book—or visit www.agilemanager.com.

Contents

Other Books in the Agile Manager Series™:

Chapter One

*F*ocus on the Reader

The Agile Manager sat silently as William, one of his product designers, made a pitch. The Agile Manager's product-development team was seeing if it could scare up some revenue by taking on some development work for other companies.

"I've got fifteen years in this business," droned William. "And the others on the team have at least as much experience as I do." The president of the company being pitched shifted in her seat uncomfortably. "I don't think there's anything we can't do." The Agile Manager winced; the president noticed.

"Thank you for stopping by, gentlemen," she said as she stood up.

"I'll put all of this in writing for you," said William. He remained seated. "Then we can get together again. How does next week sound?" William looked pleased with himself.

"Uh, I'll have to consult my planner and get back to you," she said blandly.

The Agile Manager sprang up and said, "Thank you very much for taking the time to see us. We'll be in touch." He tapped William on the shoulder and headed out the door.

*   *   *

"Hey, that was great, don't you think?" said William. "I'll bet

5

she calls us this afternoon." The Agile Manager scanned the vast parking lot for his car and said nothing. There it is, he thought.
Seated in the car, the Agile Manager said, "William, we need to talk before you write a letter to her, OK?"
"Oh—you don't think she'll call us before I have to write her?" The Agile Manager smiled. "No."

You are sitting at your computer in your office, preparing to write a critical sales letter to a prospect, Paula Wilson. You read about her in a trade journal. You know there's a good chance that an effective letter could interest Ms. Wilson in learning more about your company and the services you can provide her. You're eager to move the selling process along.

Now what? You have arrived at the point where most business professionals find themselves often. The project:

- Is within your scope of ability
- Is well worth your time
- Includes the pressure of potential failure.

Like most people, you turn to your computer, click up the word processing program, and stare at the blank screen, waiting for that magic opening to whisper itself in your ear so you can get started. But it's not coming. Your brain feels shut tight. Time for some coffee.

Back at the keyboard, you start to worry a bit. You mentally back up, take a few deep breaths. OK, OK. This isn't so tough. Let's think of a good way into this. Ahh, here's one.

What will interest your reader the most? Of course! You already know the answer. The letter opens up in front of you like a highway after driving through a tunnel. You take a grateful sigh of relief and get started.

You talk about yourself. About your company. About your product or service.

Now you are writing furiously, gradually getting caught up in the heat of how perfectly your company fits her needs. It's going well. You're writing down every possible way your company is the exact right answer for her.

She's going to love this, right? Sadly, no.

The odds are good that your reader cares nothing about you or the services you offer. She may already have people to provide those things, and she may be vaguely satisfied with their work.

Even more likely, she is overworked and understaffed. She has little or no time for an unsolicited sales pitch from you. Should your letter miraculously make it past her administrative assistant, she will probably glance at the first sentence, notice the dense paragraphs, check the signature to be sure she doesn't know you, and toss it away.

Now here's the good news. You can change this scenario into positive action if you learn the skills of other professional business writers like you.

Are you a professional writer? My rule of thumb: If you spend as little as one or two hours of your work day writing, then you need to think of yourself as a professional writer. Part of your salary is for your professional writing skill. That kind of change in attitude will help you bring about a change in your writing style.

Everyone Resists Change

In addition to being the creative director of an advertising agency, I teach business writing workshops around the U.S. and Canada.★ When I tell people at the start of the workshop that I hope they'll change the way they write, they stare at me in wide-

---

★I've been fortunate to be an instructor with Better Communications, Inc., founded by Deborah Dumaine. It is a Lexington, Massachusetts–based writing/training organization considered a leader in the field. Much of what I know about teaching business professionals to write effective documents stems from that experience.

Over several years I also taught (with a wonderful writer, the late Nancy Bolick) an on-going series of business-writing workshops at Endicott College in Beverly, Massachusetts. We developed our own workbook for that series.

eyed panic. They'd rather have root canal surgery than alter the etched-in-marble format they grew up with.

After reviewing the writing of a wide range of business professionals, I can state with some confidence that this is the document format most prefer:

—Background
—About Me
—More Background
—More About Me
—A Little About You
—My Best Idea

To make readers jump over even more hurdles right from the start, many writers begin an important letter this way:

Best Tip

If you spend as little as an hour a day writing, think of yourself as a professional writer.

"I want to take a few moments of your time to tell you about . . ."

Why do so many savvy business professionals insist on beginning with "I," the deadliest word of all? They wouldn't begin talking about themselves in a prospect's office, would they? More to the point, why are hard-charging managers and sales representatives—who understand what kind of effort it takes to stay ahead—so reluctant to jettison their clunky, shopworn writing style in favor of a leaner, more efficient model?

Here's the best answer I can come up with. It would be a betrayal of Miss Grundy or Mr. Peepers, or whoever the teacher was who first taught them composition in ninth grade.

That's it. After years of cajoling people to change, I'm convinced that the image of a junior-high English teacher is so embedded in their minds that it takes lengthy training and sharp motivation to move them into a new way of thinking.

Consider this: If you were in ninth grade in the 1970s, then your teacher probably graduated from college in the early 1970s or late 1960s. He or she used textbooks written in the early 1960s or late 1950s. The authors based those texts on principles of what constituted good writing from the 1930s or 1940s. That was:

- Twenty years before electric typewriters
- Forty years before desktop computers
- Fifty years before affordable fax machines, modems, the Internet, and e-mail.

The Pace of Change Quickens

Since the Baby Boomers were born, the world has undergone sweepingly dramatic changes in the ways we think and create and communicate. In this era of instant communication, old-fashioned ways of writing are deadly.

The crush of today's important business writing includes:

- Memos
- Cold sales letters
- Warm prospect letters
- Reports
- Proposals
- Meeting minutes.

Our writing styles must change to meet such a challenge. Competition, I believe, enhanced by the ubiquitous power of desktop computing, has altered the nature of the workforce and the way we all do business. Anyone on the planet who can afford a computer is now your potential competitor, whether you make running shoes or sell web-design services. Chaos has replaced status quo. Just keeping up has replaced getting ahead.

People are totally focused now on maximizing their efforts

Best Tip

Conjure up an image of all your English teachers. Thank them for a job well done— then dismiss them. For good.

simply to stay in place and not slide backwards. That's why there is so little time to devote to a document from you or from anyone else. And that's why, when prospects and customers do find that precious nanosecond to devote to a piece of writing from you, it has to hit the target immediately.

The day the world changed for me. In 1986, I was into my second year of being a freelance writer. Several clients were pressuring me to invest in some equipment that would save them time in working with me. So I bought my first fax machine. It cost a cool $600. It used thermal paper, the kind that curls up like a peeled onion skin.

The same day I installed the fax machine, a longtime client called, a producer at an advertising agency, with a video script project for me. I shared the good news that I was fax-ready.

"Good," she said. "We have a tight deadline on this project. Now you can fax me each page as you write it."

With one purchase I had suddenly managed to trim the time I had to think and polish down to zero. Time, once my ally, now was my enemy.

If you're like me, you no longer have the luxury of taking a week to create and edit an effective writing project. Now we are all down to days, sometimes even hours.

Best Tip

Your writing—whether memo, letter, report, or proposal— must hit the mark immediately. Your readers have no time to wade through your words.

The pace of business isn't the only thing that has changed. The audience has changed as well. Your readers are different today than they were ten years ago.

Many still think of America as a product economy, with the standard do-things-one-at-a-time attitude that works on the shop floor. But America is a service economy, according to *American Demographics* (May 1996). In 1970, 32 percent of us worked in goods-producing industries. Now it's 15 percent. More than eight in ten Americans work in service jobs such as transportation, retail, and finance. People must do several activities in a tight time frame and can in no way devote full attention to any document from you.

Everyone Is Overloaded

If there's simply too much to read in this brave new computerized world of ours, there's also too much to write.

The home office requires documentation for everything. Pharmaceutical sales representatives, to cite one industry, must keep voluminous records of sales calls just to avoid lawsuits. And someone has to maintain notes of meetings, don't they? What about that growing pile of e-mail? Who is going to answer the messages arriving daily on the Web site?

Remember the glowing predictions about the Paperless Office? Didn't happen. Never will. Human beings need to hold a piece of paper in their hands in order to think of the subject as "real." You might think about investing in tree farms.

Business Week wrote a few years ago that a Boeing 747 could not fly while carrying the paperwork necessary for its construction. Others have suggested that there is more information in today's edition of *The New York Times* than people living in the sixteenth century needed to know in their lifetimes.

Please remember the one universal constant about business writing in this era of electronic marvels: Your reader doesn't have enough time to do everything he or she needs to do.

When you write a document to busy readers you are in effect asking them to donate to you a portion of their time. They know they will have to make up that time later on. That's why they will not permit you and me to waste it.

The paper flood. Businesses around the globe are losing the fight against the flow of paper. There's no stopping it. I'll bet that fewer than half of all the documents that cross your desk every day get so much as a cursory glance. How many do you take the time to read and study? Ten percent? Fifteen percent?

If that's true for you, it's also true for the person you're trying to reach by writing.

If you're going to take the trouble to learn a new writing style, it helps to know that the Old Rules have changed.

Out with the Old, In with the New

Here are some of those Old Rules. If any of them describes the way you think about writing today, you probably have a ninth-grade English teacher to thank for it. (I suspect, however, that if your teacher were standing next to you as you write a business document today, he or she would advise you to be as effective as possible.) With apologies to Miss Bingham, my own guide to junior-high grammar, I've included some of the New Rules in brief here. I'll discuss them further and give examples later.

Old Rule #1: Begin with background.

Load up your readers with as many facts, figures, and history as you can gather and make them suffer. After all, you suffered while researching all that information, so it's only fair to make your readers suffer too.

Here's the catch. You had no choice but to amass all this data. It is part of your job. But your readers do not consider it part of their job to suffer with you.

Academic style is not business style. You will recognize this emphasis on background first if you've ever written a graduate thesis or college term paper. It is classic academic style. Build argument on argument in logical, persuasive fashion so that your reader can't help agreeing with you when you (finally) get to the point. This works in academia for two reasons:

1. Teachers and professors like this style.
2. They get paid to read it.

Outside of your own company, your readers have bosses who expect them to perform, not to read something from you. They have neither the time nor the patience to wade through multiple paragraphs of background. After all, how do they know that the payoff is worth their time?

New Rule: Background belongs in back. If you simply must include background, don't let it interfere with what's new and fresh. Put it at the end or in an attachment.

Old Rule #2: Write long, complex paragraphs.

In almost all of your academic writing, junior high through graduate school, your objective was to demonstrate the depth of your learning in dense paragraphs using complex words.

This is fine. Complex ideas deserve complex writing and sophisticated vocabulary.

Your instructors, for their part, had a similar agenda. They wanted to discern the quality of your thinking by the density of your thoughts and the level of vocabulary you employ to express those thoughts. This is fair.

Write short sentences and use short words. Your readers have time for nothing else.

What's not fair is to expect the same quality of interest from business readers, who tend to be far more casual and much busier than their academic counterparts when it comes to reading your prose.

A few years ago Robert J. Samuelson, the M.I.T. economist, wrote an article on macroeconomics. Nothing special about that, except that he used words no longer than two syllables, just to show that it is possible. If he can do it on a subject so arcane as macroeconomics, so can you.

New Rule: Use the shortest word possible to get the job done. Write short, concise paragraphs, no longer than five or six typed lines. While you're at it, write short sentences, too.

Old Rule #3: Write in thesis style with no subheads to show sequence.

I've heard people from the Old School say headlines or subheads in writing are inappropriate for conservative organizations. Just keep your paragraphs dedicated to a topic sentence, they say, and the ideas that flow from that topic. Use transitions here and there, and—voilà!—you'll have hard-working prose.

This notion has credence, along with hundreds of years of scholarly history behind it. The ideas speak for themselves; the writer simply has to set them down in classic paragraph style. Did F. Scott Fitzgerald need subheads? St. Thomas Aquinas? No. So why then do you?

While this format may be useful for scholars, who tend to read with slow intensity, it in no way reflects the hour-by-hour changing crises of a contemporary business office. From meetings to phone calls to meetings and airports and more meetings, today's harried executives are looking for any excuse to dump all nonessential or hard-to-read documents into the trash and get on with it.

You have to win readership. Your document may in fact contain essential information. But unless you give readers a clear idea of the structure of your ideas and relevance to them right from the start, they will miss it in the haste of daily business life.

Best Tip

Win readers by showing, from the start, why your ideas are relevant to them.

It might help, in deciding whether subheads are right for you, to compare audio cassettes with compact disks. Cassettes are like the Old Rules with their linear format. To find a certain cut of music you want to hear means forwarding, testing, rewinding, testing, until you get close. With a digital-format CD, however, a listener can go to any cut instantly.

Similarly, good business writing describes each section so readers can immediately find the ideas that interest them the most. Avoid making readers scan up and down a document in a frustrating attempt to find out exactly what it is you want from them.

New Rule: Use subheads lavishly. Include an action verb in most of them.

Old Rule #4: Save your most important idea until the end.

This, too, is straight from the academic style book. It has about it the importance of drama. Othello doesn't die until the last act. Odysseus is not reunited with Penelope until the final few stanzas. Indiana Jones doesn't save the world until just before the credits.

This is fine and appropriate for drama, where the writer expects members of the audience to do nothing but sit there and watch passively. A business document is not drama; you expect it to incite action. Therefore you cannot use the tools of literature to get action, a purpose for which literature is spectacularly unsuited.

Best Tip

Incite action—always your goal—by putting your main idea up front.

Attention first, then action. Action happens only when you first get attention. In business, that means hitting the reader right from the start with the importance of your best idea.

Tip: There are some occasions when you might want to delay getting to your main point. Conveying bad news is one example, or preparing readers for a price that's higher than they expected. Such instances require sensitivity and judgment, especially in the opening paragraphs. For the great majority of the time, however, get right to the point and make it loud and clear.

New Rule: Begin with your main idea most of the time.

In the next chapter, you'll find out exactly how to do it.

Hold Your Horses

At this point, I hope you're excited about new possibilities for that first draft.

But wait.

Before you reach for the keyboard, you need to take some valuable time to prepare to be effective.

Successful business writers—the ones who make the sale, the ones who get promoted into better positions at a higher salary—take time to think before they write. Your best ideas need nurturing and a clear sense of direction if they're going to have a chance to work.

It's like painting your house.

Inexperienced painters climb up the ladder and start dabbing on the paint. Then next year they get to watch as the paint peels off in sheets and the house looks worse than before.

Good painters work hardest at preparing for the job. They replace rotten boards, scrape, sand, wash, prime, and caulk. Then they paint.

It's also like taking a studio photograph. Good photographers are glad to spend nearly all of the work in preparation, posing the model just right, making the lighting perfect, testing and retesting. Taking the actual photograph involves less than one second of time.

If you do the prep work properly, you'll find that writing the draft is the easiest part of the whole process. So let's get started—on preparing to write.

The Agile Manager's Checklist

✔ Be prepared to give up your long-held, cherished ideas of what constitutes good writing. Inciting the reader to action requires a new set of rules.

✔ Put your main idea at the top of the document. Readers are too busy to wade through it to find your purpose.

✔ Use subheads. They make good guideposts for readers.

Chapter Two

To Get Action, Get Attention

"I know you said to talk to you before writing Lynn Halsey," said William as he bounced into the Agile Manager's office. *"But you've been tied up in meetings all day. So I wrote a letter anyway."* He handed the Agile Manager a sheet of paper.

"Dear Lynn," the letter began. *"I'm glad we had the chance to tell you about our capabilities as product developers and designers. As I mentioned, there's no one better than us in this business. Last year, for instance, we won three design awards. And I was the lead designer on a product that sold 35,000 units! . . ."*

The Agile Manager put the letter down. He suppressed his urge to send William a message by tearing up the letter. "William," he said, "we need to start at the beginning here. First of all, that meeting yesterday didn't go very well. I can tell you right now that she probably wants nothing to do with us."

"What? I don't believe that. I told her all about us and how good we were. And—"

"That's exactly right, Willie," said the Agile Manager with a grin. "You did a great job telling her how good we are." His eyebrows twitched as he said, "But you never told her how we could help her. You never asked what her needs are."

"What do you mean? She knows what we're capable of. She can fit us into her plans." William looked defiant.

The Agile Manager lost his patience. He reached into his desk and pulled out a piece of paper that said "Planning Guide" at the top. "Make a copy of this and fill it out. Then let's talk."

What's the best way to get anyone's attention? Plan for it.

Getting the reader's attention is not part of the mindset of most business writers today. It should be. After all, you're competing with a myriad of distractions, from an unexpected crisis to a coffee break to the telephone ringing to the 3:00 P.M. status meeting.

Grab the reader's attention up front and don't let it go until you've accomplished your purpose.

Planning Guide: A Solid Basis for Powerful Writing

All lasting structures begin with a solid foundation. In writing, that foundation is your clear understanding of what it is you're trying to accomplish and why the reader should be interested.

Forward-thinking companies from ad agencies to aircraft builders have used a document similar to the one on the following page in the first phase of planning. Whether you call it a "creative platform" or "project description," everyone involved needs to be clear on exactly what the purpose is.

The Planning Guide outlines the basic issues you should describe—in writing—before beginning any project. I recommend you type it permanently into your hard drive and fill it in before beginning every document, presentation, or important phone call. (You can also enlarge my version on a photocopier.)

Let's examine each of these guidelines:

1. The main reason I am writing this is to _____.

Answer this in the reader's terms. An answer in your terms is not productive. You're off track if you fill in the blank with an answer such as:

Planning Guide

1. The main reason I am writing this is to_____
    _____
    _____
    _____.

2. The problem the reader has that I can solve or help
    to solve is _____
    _____
    _____
    _____.

3. The action I want the reader to take is _____
    _____
    _____
    _____.

4. My most important reader-centered idea is_____
    _____
    _____
    _____
    _____.

5. The reader's two most-critical professional con-
    cerns are _____
    _____
    _____
    _____.

6. The reader's likely reaction to my ideas will be
    <u>POSITIVE</u>   <u>NEUTRAL</u>   <u>NEGATIVE</u> (circle one).

- To make a sale
- To keep my job
- To earn a bonus
- To fulfill a direct assignment.

Those may be the actual reasons behind your writing energy, but they're unhelpful as far as getting action is concerned. The reader doesn't care about anything from your perspective. So put the answer in reader-centered action words. Examples:

. . . demonstrate to the customer the advantages of a working relationship with me.

. . . notify customers of a product change that will result in long-term sales.

. . . make amends for a customer-relations incident we botched last week.

Notice that a weak answer such as "I want my reader to be informed" won't do here. Being informed is not action. Don't inform people. Motivate them.

2. The problem the reader has that I can solve or help to solve is _____.

If you can't solve some kind of problem for readers, why are you taking their time? Why should they be interested in anything you have to say otherwise? Answer this as concretely as you can, and you have a good chance of success. If nothing else, answering this question might point you to gaps in your research that need filling.

3. The action I want the reader to take is _____.

Examples: pencil an appointment into her calendar; mail me a check; call me with follow-up questions.

If you can visualize the reader doing some form of physical action, you have a chance to make it happen.

4. My most important reader-centered idea is _____.

This is payload thinking at its most strategic. If you do not have a single main idea, then you cannot create a strategic document that will drive action.

5. **The reader's two most-critical professional concerns are** _____.

Examples: increased competition; lack of time to perform successfully; diminishing returns from a mailing list; reduction in product quality; employee turnover.

If you don't know the answer, make your best guess or do more research.

6. **The reader's likely reaction to my ideas will be** POSITIVE   NEUTRAL   NEGATIVE.

Your main idea always goes at the beginning of the document, unless the reader is likely to react negatively. If so, place the main idea in a more appropriate place, but never at the end.

For this line, I advise people to assume the worst. If the reader might be positive, assume neutral. If the reader might be neutral, assume negative. Don't be nervous about a neutral reader. Neutral is good! Most readers are neutral; that is, they are disinterested yet open to a good idea if it comes their way. So give them the good idea up front.

How to Get Attention

Getting attention is the only skill in business writing that borders on art.

Let's look at how artists grab attention, and perhaps learn from it.

Take the movies. Remember *Men In Black*? Does it begin with five minutes of explication, telling us that there are aliens living among us, some benign and some dangerous? Not a bit. But isn't that background important for understanding the story? Maybe, but not just yet. What's immediately important is that we care about these two men in black. We'll get the background in due time.

Right now the producers want to yank us into the action, and so we begin with a foot chase. Here we are, racing down a Manhattan street with a young cop, trying to catch up with a thug who seems to have superhuman strength. There are turns, crashes, jumps, and a building frustration on the part of the policeman. Who could resist coming along for the ride? Let's move up a bit on the cultural scale and go to the theater. The curtain opens on foggy ramparts centuries ago. The guards are talking about the decay of empire and . . . ghosts. Something's rotten in Denmark, and off we go with Prince Hamlet on a verbal whirlwind. Who could resist?

Then there's Mozart, the master of attention-grabbing. *The Marriage of Figaro*, for instance, opens with a man on his hands and knees measuring his room for a bed. Not your standard opera opening. Listen to virtually any of Mozart's smaller instrumental pieces and you'll discover he begins with the full power and excitement of his main theme.

Down on the day-to-day level where we live, the best way to get someone's attention is to ask about what interests him or her. Your interest, if genuine, will astonish them and give you the advantage.

I like what Barbara Walters recommends in her excellent book, *How to Talk with Practically Anybody About Practically Anything.* Most people have at least one or two genuinely interesting aspects of their personalities, and just a little digging will bring it out. In turn, they will think you're a fascinating conversationalist.

Tools to Get Attention

The Planning Guide, while an excellent way to start, isn't the whole story. It's likely going to take more than one key idea to motivate a reader. You may need a whole bunch to do the job. Where are those ideas going to come from?

Further, you may need time and hard research to generate ideas that will turn the tide in your favor.

(Please note: This is a digression on how to use some psychological "tricks" to enhance your creativity. If you already have all the ideas you need, please skip ahead to the next chapter.)

Here are five tools that, like shovels and flashlights, will help you search for the ideas that will best appeal to readers and grab their attention from the start:

- Brainstorming
- Mindmapping
- Index Cards
- Questioning
- Field Research

First: Understand How Your Mind Works

Psychiatrists have devoted a century of study to determine how the mind works. Scientifically, we have only scratched the surface.

The latest research shows that the brain is infinitely more complex than we thought even a few years ago. Research on accident victims, for example, suggests a regenerative power in the brain that surpasses our wildest estimates. It remains for future researchers to open up new vistas regarding the power and complexity of the human brain.

For us now, however, there are several practical insights into how the brain works that we can turn into tools that help us attract attention and write more effectively.

Put the Left Brain/Right Brain Theory to use. A generation ago, psychologists were excited about this new model of how the human brain works. It became known as the Left Brain/Right Brain Theory. Since then, researchers have moved away from this theory as too simplistic. As a model for understanding writing behavior, however, it still offers good guidance.

|Best Tip

Identify a specific problem a reader has. How can you solve it? There's the basis for a letter or memo.

To simplify, the theory states that all human beings enjoy the power of a brain that performs essentially two conflicting—but necessary—functions. For convenience, call these the Right Brain and Left Brain.

Half of our mind's power is devoted to cognitive skills, such as reasoning, mathematics, logical process—the "hard" abilities, which we may think of as occupying the left side.

The other (right side) half of our thinking power involves the "soft" abilities such as emotion, creativity, the arts, and love.

All human beings participate in both sides of this mental coin. Mechanical engineers, for example, while pursuing clearly left-brain careers, have been known to fall in love and write sonnets with right brain skill. Many famous writers, from Chaucer to Hawthorne to Thomas Clancy, have pursued right-brain creative outlets while performing left-brain jobs such as accounting, customs house recording, or actuarial insurance.

Best Tip

Watch 'Star Trek' a few times to understand how the different parts of the brain work—and how you can employ this knowledge profitably.

In cases of physical damage to the brain, we can see the results of one side taking precedence over the other, such as severely mentally impaired individuals who can play classical violin or break the casino in blackjack.

Logical versus Romantic. As a memory key, think of left (L) as Logical and right (R) as Romantic. Now let's look at how this theory provides a practical way to get our brains to generate ideas.

The best way I know of to start is to consider the old "Star Trek" television series.

Many people find it amazing that a television idea from the late 1960s simply will not go away, but instead keeps expanding into ever more TV and movie ideas.

I believe the old series was a perfect depiction of how our brains work. "Star Trek" is a model of you and me! Let's check it out.

Who represented the cold, logical side of human thinking? First Officer Spock, of course. He would calmly count down the seconds to disaster, seemingly unable to imagine what that disaster would feel like.

Who speaks for the warm, emotional side of human thought? Doctor McCoy, naturally. The essence of the series was that these two were constantly bickering and contradicting each other—just as we all experience the conflict of logic and emotion within ourselves. To me, the original "Star Trek" was successful because it embodied the warring aspects of human nature, the continuing struggle (to throw Freud into the mix) between our bloodthirsty ids and ballet-loving superegos.

How we stay on course. What about Captain Kirk's role? He was vital. He was the physical symbol of those two opposing natures within one human being. Because he participates fully in both logic and emotion, he is the perfect choice to command the ship on course among the stars.

What has all this "Star Trek" explication to do with writing? Well, if you understand that you have two warring natures within yourself, each vying for attention and ascendancy, you're able to understand what happens when one side of you wants to create and one side wants to edit—at the same time. You can't do it.

The trick in creating anything is to give your logical side permission to go away for a while, so the emotional side is able to do its work.

Coming up with attention-grabbing ideas and then writing the first draft are warm (emotional) tasks. Evaluating, editing, and rewriting are cold (logical) tasks. The two can't operate together. One must follow the other.

Best Tip
First, create with abandon. Then let your left brain (the logical side) take over to edit and analyze.

If you're trying to write but the ideas won't come, chances are you're trying to be both logical and emotional at the same time. You need a tool that will trick your brain into saying, OK, I'm going to be creative for now, then logical later. The brain, fortunately, is easily fooled if you know how to do it.

Try Brainstorming

The best tool I know of to dismiss your logical side while welcoming your creative side is brainstorming. It gives logic permission to go away.

What is it?

Brainstorming: The methodical search of your sub-conscious mind for ideas while in a state of relaxed, positive creativity.

There are only two rules in brainstorming:

1. Go for quantity, not quality. Your aim is to capture every relevant idea in the universe. So get them all down—good, bad, silly, indifferent, impossible, outrageous, funny. One idea always leads to another. The more ideas, the more comfortable you'll be that you can distill them down to strong elements for an effective document.

2. Every idea is a good idea. This is a necessary condition to success. By disallowing negativity or criticism, you are encouraging your mind to let the ideas flow. And flow they will.

Brainstorming works best in a group of ten or fewer individuals who have committed to about thirty minutes of creative time together. One idea caroms off another as everyone gets into the act. Someone should take notes or write the ideas as they occur on a notepad or—best of all—a flip chart for all to see. Since brainstorming is open-ended, so should the notes be.

The best format is a "spider web" with the main purpose as its center and branches radiating infinitely out from it.

Because every idea is a good idea, positive energy can crackle in the room as people become more creative, even more playful.

Brainstorm alone. If necessary, you can also brainstorm alone, sitting in front of your computer or a note pad. While not as fun as in a group, it can be just as productive.

Here are my brainstorming notes before writing this section:

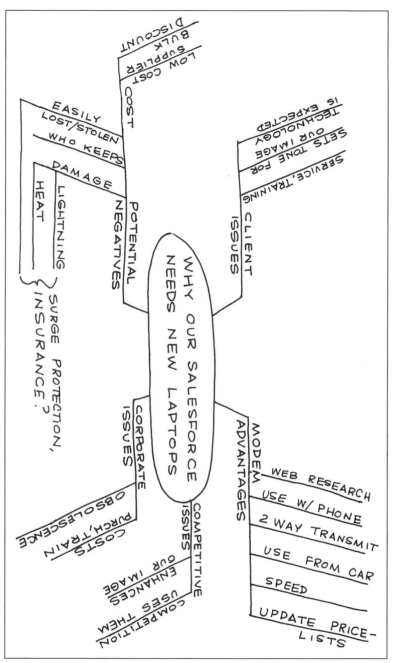

**A brainstorming diagram from
an actual strategy session**

General Intro.
Example or 2
Dr. Land
Star Trek
solo
mindmapping as specific case
effectiveness?
how creativity works
mental elevator—Kirby Who?
spider web
good energizing wrap to inspire reader

What's this note about Dr. Land? He's a prime example of why you should consider any idea as valid, no matter how silly or irrelevant it may seem at the time.

Creating a new industry. According to his biography, Dr. Edwin Land was vacationing in Arizona with his family, back in the late 1940s. He and his young daughter took a walk in the desert one afternoon, and Dr. Land was dutifully taking snapshots of the landscape with his trusty Brownie camera.

His daughter, six or seven years old, at one point asked, "Daddy, when can we see the pictures?"

He explained that it would be some time. First they had to walk back to town, he would drop off the film at the druggist's store, and the druggist would mail the film to New York for processing. Then someone would mail him the photos. In all, perhaps six weeks.

A childish question. "Why can't we see the pictures now?" she asked. A perfectly naive question from an inexperienced source. Instead of laughing, Dr. Land thought about that childish question for months. In coming up with a solution, he founded a new industry, instant photography, and a new company, Polaroid.

There are dozens of other examples of seemingly dumb questions that led directly to brilliant solutions. In the heat of brainstorming, no one can distinguish a good idea from a poor idea, so don't even try. Write them all down. Keep the atmosphere positive and electric. You will be amazed at what comes out of a session like that.

Mindmapping

Mindmapping is a visually oriented, new-age cousin to brain-storming. Tony Buzan is generally credited with coining the word in the 1970s. It's based on the premise that one remembers images easier and longer than words. In its purest form it involves a series of sketches, one leading to another, in an attempt to free your mind of its normal word-bound restrictions. It reveals the "shapes" of your ideas and shows how they relate to each other. As a way of telling the brain to relax and let the ideas flow, it is superb. It helps to have an artistic flair.

Guidelines for mindmapping:

1. Make the central idea a strong visual image;
2. Use icons or visuals whenever possible in place of words;
3. Think of the process as a journey;
4. Use color to trace the direction of distinct themes;
5. Practice letting your mind relax;
6. Expect to have fun. Creativity is a function of play—as any child will be glad to tell you.

I find mindmapping to be an excellent way to prepare for a speech or other presentation. A quick glance at your mindmap tells you instantly where you are and where you're going. Compared to speaking from dense written notes, it is a breeze. Try using a mindmap rather than notes to produce a seamless speech.

Put your mind on cruise control. People who like mind-mapping say it induces the same feeling as driving on a lonely highway, where the subconscious brain attends to driving while the conscious brain wanders where it will. Suddenly, you're five miles down the road with no idea how you got there.

In Left Brain/Right Brain terms, you are stepping outside of the verbal box (L) and opening up whole new visual (R) vistas.

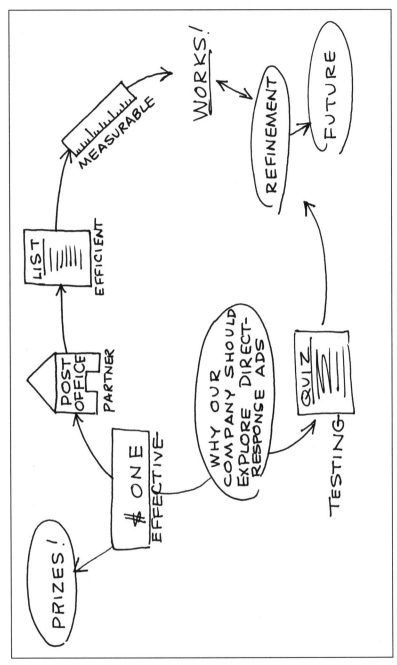

A mindmapping diagram, also from an actual strategy session

Exercises such as mindmapping relax your mind. Reflections in tranquillity, as the poet William Wordsworth put it, is a favored state of the creative brain. Ideas seem to float into view, like corks on a pond, when the brain is tranquil. That's why some of your best ideas will occur in the middle of the night as you awake from a dream, or while doing some familiar activity, like taking a shower, for which your brain requires little attention.

Another way to look at it. My brain sometimes feels divided into left and right. Mostly, however, it feels as if there's a factory on the main floor and a reference library down deep in the basement.

The factory is open all day and all evening. Ideas, input, sensations, stimuli, come in and go out constantly. Once in a while I'll see or hear something that stops the flow. Maybe I see an actor in a movie on television, and say to my wife, "Look, honey, that guy. What's his name? You know. He always plays a city guy, has a unique voice." My wife, who hates television, might look up from her book and say "Don't know."

Ask the librarian. So then—and this is the good part—I'll make a little mental note and send it via pneumatic tube to the little guy who works all alone in the library downstairs.

"What's the name of that actor, smart-aleck, character type, Herbert, Kerburt, Sherbert Something, did *City Slickers* with Billy Crystal?"

Then I'll go to bed relaxed, assured that someone is working on it. The little guy in the library, meanwhile, is up all night, looking through the files. Come 3:00 A.M., when I'm up raiding the 'fridge for a snack that invariably isn't there, the message tube pops back up on the factory floor and there's a note from the little guy:

"Bruno Kirby."

That's how my brain works, and probably yours too. Knowing it, and planning for it, is how professionals demystify the process of writing.

You can't force ideas. The trick is to stop trying to *force* your mind to work and let it operate naturally, in tranquillity. That sense of peacefulness can come from sleep or dreams, or you can induce it with techniques such as brainstorming, mindmapping, or some of the other methods below.

Where do ideas come from? They come from you, from the accumulation of your life's experiences and reading, from your family life, from the experiences of your friends. Ideas occur mostly when your brain is in a relaxed state.

Use Index Cards

Using index cards is a tactile technique that works wonders. I find simple physical pleasure in using index cards, especially the larger 5-by-7-inch ones, and that translates into a relaxed creative state.

Let's say you have an important proposal to write—a long one, complex, with lots riding on the outcome. Your mind's first impulse is to panic, but pay no attention to it. Instead, take out a stack of index cards. Think of several of the most important elements your proposal must contain. Write them on the cards, one element per card.

You'll soon discover that your mind likes this technique. Relaxation comes with enjoyment. As you mentally push panic aside and begin to enjoy the process, other ideas or elements will come to mind. Write them down on individual cards as well.

Now spread out the cards with notes on them all over your desk or table. Keep jotting down ideas. They will come fast for fifteen or twenty minutes, then slow quickly. That's your signal that your brain doesn't have much left in that particular closet.

It's time to go back to the ideas on individual cards and begin filling in the important details that go with each idea. You'll find this, too, starts to flow well, then dries up. Fine. Take a break.

When you come back to the project, begin to put the cards in some kind of order. The order could be anything, but it should be based on what the reader is looking for or will find most useful. For example:

- Most important to least important
- Most recent to earliest
- Most expensive to least expensive.

Keep moving the cards around until the order feels right. Suddenly, you have a structure—without even turning on the computer. **Avoid left-brain activities in this stage.** At this point you might feel confident enough to start writing the first draft. But don't. Your creative side has more preparations to take care of first. Further, once you turn on the computer, your left brain starts to take over. Your logical side feels compelled to be orderly and is predisposed to interrupt creative free-flow. That's why I've given you several exercises that take place off-line, while your mind is still likely to be calm and fertile with ideas.

Put your ideas on index cards, then arrange them according to your purpose. It's a method that can work wonders.

Index cards are useful not only as idea generators, but also as an excellent format for large projects. I've had good success with them on 80-page proposals, eight-hour workshop presentations, and 120-page screenplays. They're the only format I know that allows the writer to see the scope of the entire project at once, even if you have to spread the cards out on the floor to see them all.

Like other kinds of cards, you can shuffle them into any order you like, indefinitely. Try them once, and you'll probably keep a fresh blank deck in your briefcase at all times. They're that useful. Many people have had similar success with Post-it Notes®.

Employ Questioning

The most popular idea-generating technique in workshops, besides brainstorming, is questioning. In its essence, it is a way for you quickly to put yourself imaginatively in the reader's shoes. By telling your brain that you are now looking at life as the reader looks at it, you'll discover whole new perspectives that were formerly closed to you.

As a direct-mail copywriter friend of mine says, "You may be selling grass seed, but I'm buying a beautiful lawn." That's looking at life from the reader's (customer's) perspective.

Here's how questioning works:

1. *Start with your purpose for writing.* Example: The reason I'm writing this is to get my readers to schedule me on their calendars for a one-on-one office visit.

2. *On a few fresh pieces of paper, list the top ten questions your reader would ask, if he or she could, about your purpose.* Underline each question. Leave lots of space between questions. I've picked ten as a realistic number. Five might do. Or fifteen. Some examples:

   "Why is a face-to-face meeting important?"

   "Why do you think I'm a good prospect for your product/service?"

   "I'm already using a product/service similar to yours. Why should I switch?"

   "I've never heard of your company before, so why should I waste my time?"

   "What's the most important reason I should be interested in your product/service?"

   "Do you even know the central problem getting in my way?"

   "Why does your service come with the highest price of all your competitors?"

3. *Once you've asked all the really compelling questions, go back and answer them briefly in short, bulleted points.*

I hope you'll discover, as most workshop participants do, that your document now has form and substance—all that remains is to fill in the gaps using format techniques I'll show you later.

Now the hard part is over. You've already done the hardest part of writing business documents, namely, looking at the issues from the reader's perspective rather than your own. This is the most creative use of imagination for most writers. The rest is simply drawing from your own knowledge to convince the reader that you have his or her best interests in mind.

Please try questioning, even if only for a few minutes. I've heard many people say it is the one technique missing from their skills, and the single most effective way to approach selling from a "you" perspective.

Research

Nothing on earth matches hard-slogging field research as the writer's most formidable tool for discovering the right ideas to get attention and make that sale, whether a product to a customer or an idea to a supervisor.

Here's an example of what I mean by field research. A metal-products (sheaves, ball bearings, etc.) manufacturing company in the South once hired me to write a corporate video. They showed me their facilities and old bro-

Best Tip

Do research to come up with ideas that make the sale. It's your most formidable tool.

chures and said go write something. I asked for permission to access their archives, since I read in one of the brochures that the company was over one hundred years old.

The client thought the request was unusual but liked it the more he thought about it. He took me to another building where the company kept archival records. I felt as if I had walked into that final scene from *Raiders of the Lost Ark*, where thousands of crates stand piled on top of each other in a warehouse.

I finally found the earliest records and started there. After about six hours, I discovered that the original company, a wooden-jack maker supplying the covered-wagon trains out of Ohio, had burned to the ground in the 1880s. The proprietor, smart fellow, rebuilt a bigger plant to make iron jacks instead of wood. And prospered ever after.

So right then I wrote a theme for the company that is still going strong: "Born in Fire."

On the simplest level, the company forges its metal products in extreme heat. On a deeper level, its reputation for adapting to new challenges was born in the flames of that first plant. I had come up with a winner, but only because I was willing to get my hands dirty doing all the research necessary.

The answers are out there, and not at your desk. This is true for every business writer. The answers that will provide you with selling ideas are in the marketplace, where what you're selling grinds against what people need every day.

Insistence on firsthand field research has taken me from a Federal penitentiary in South Carolina to a Tennessee morgue, from volunteering in a do-it-yourself blood-test experiment in Boston to interviewing people about their sore throats in Seattle, the sore-throat capital of America.

If doing field research is an option for you, do it. Offer to work in a prospect's place of business for a week or two. If you're selling industrial ovens, try to work in a cafeteria or a jail. If you're selling luggage, go to a few baggage-handling operations in airports. If you're selling cereal, go join a few dozen families at the breakfast table. If you're selling health insurance, go hang out in a few hospitals. If you're selling corporate software, go live with the clients for a few days and see what their needs really are.

Following are three examples of good field research from the advertising industry.

1. Volkswagen

Possibly the best print ad in history is the one for Volkswagen that Doyle Dane Bernbach, then a powerhouse advertising agency, created in the 1960s.

It features a photo of a Volkswagen "Beetle" and this large, one-word headline below it: **Lemon.**

Going directly against the category called "Car Advertising," this ad launched Volkswagen into the popular culture where the company stayed until it mistakenly started selling big, powerful cars.

The ad came about because some agency staffers were on a field trip to the main plant in Germany. They saw several workers pushing what looked like a perfect car off the assembly line. When asked, the tour guide said that what was wrong with the car was the final layer of paint. It had several microscopic flaws.

The agency figured correctly that drivers would love a car made with those high standards, and it came up with a creative way to tell the story. (Bill Bernbach, the creative head of the agency for many years, once suggested that the German clients approved the ad because they didn't understand what American consumers mean when they use the word "lemon" while referring to a car, but that's another story.)

My point is, they never would have come up with the idea sitting behind desks in New York. You get ideas on the shop

Lemon.

This Volkswagen missed the boat.
The chrome strip on the glove compartment is blemished and must be replaced. Chances are you wouldn't have noticed it; Inspector Kurt Kroner did.
There are 3,389 men at our Wolfsburg factory with only one job: to inspect Volkswagens at each stage of production. (3000 Volkswagens are produced daily; there are more inspectors than cars.)

Every shock absorber is tested (spot checking won't do), every windshield is scanned. VWs have been rejected for surface scratches barely visible to the eye.
Final inspection is really something! VW inspectors run each car off the line onto the Funktionsprüfstand (car test stand), tote up 189 check points, gun ahead to the automatic

brake stand, and say "no" to one VW out of fifty.
This preoccupation with detail means the VW lasts longer and requires less maintenance, by and large, than other cars. (It also means a used VW depreciates less than any other car.)
We pluck the lemons; you get the plums.

Used by permission of Volkswagen of America

floor, in suburban homes and downtown lofts, in banks and convenience stores, in places where people congregate—like cafeterias and Grange halls—where the action always lives.

2. Surf Detergent
Surf was a come-lately to the laundry detergent industry. Surf's makers studied its competitors and realized that all were telling the "brightness" story as a way to demonstrate cleanness. It didn't have enough money to compete with the big soaps on the brightness level, and so it sent lab people to Laundromats all over America, hoping to discover another way to measure clean.

Know what they found? People in Laundromats didn't care a fig about brightness. To tell whether clothes are clean, people smell them.

Surf tripled the perfume content of their soap against competitors and instantly grabbed a 12 percent share of this massive market.

3. Milk Advisory Board
Goodby Silverstein is a hot creative ad agency on the West Coast. Based on its reputation for pushing through boundaries, the people at the Milk Advisory Board hired it to persuade Americans to drink more milk.

The account executive did some quick research by asking a dozen friends and neighbors about their attitudes toward milk. The response was almost universal. People think about milk only when they are out of it.

From that vantage point, the creative department came up with what is now classic advertising: "Got milk?" The campaign is still winning awards and—more importantly—selling milk. And all this from merely talking to twelve people.

Sometimes the answers are at your desk. It helps, of course, if your desk contains a computer with a modem that allows you to tap into the Internet. The World Wide Web is already a treasure house of information. Just don't let it be your only source.

With just a few minutes of practice you can learn how to scan the Web for:

- Annual reports
- Stock and financial quotes
- Individual biographies and addresses
- Areas of expertise (such as mindmapping, which has dozens of links, like *www.thinksmart.com/productmindmapcontents.html* and *www.advanced.org/thinkquest/tqguide2/mindmapping1.html*)
- The on-line resources of libraries around the world.

To write successful documents, be prepared to use every research tool on earth, from the Internet to your local library. Don't be shy about calling up university professors or civic leaders and quizzing them if they have any knowledge at all about your topic. Most people are glad to have someone asking them for their expert opinions.

You should also have stacks of reference books in your office: dictionaries, atlas, thesaurus, books of quotations, writing handbooks, speech compilations, even joke books.

Good ideas are the only foundation for writing that gets action. The whole point of such activities as brainstorming, index card notes, and research is to build confidence. You want to convince your creative self that where your writing project is concerned, all the possible good ideas that once existed out there in the ether are now safely written down in a form that you can easily use.

Having captured those ideas, now you can move on to another vital task in the process: arranging those ideas for maximum effect.

The Agile Manager's Checklist

✔ To get attention, plan for it. Use the Planning Guide and tools like brainstorming.

✔ Most important: Offer a benefit-laden, reader-centered idea. Think in terms of "you," and not "I."

✔ Don't bother to write unless you can solve a problem.

Chapter Three

Arrange Ideas Strategically

At the end of the day, the Agile Manager stopped by William's cubicle. "How's it going?" he said.

"I think I'm beginning to see," he said slowly. "I snagged Shelly from sales for a few minutes after lunch. She really liked the Planning Guide, by the way, and made a copy herself. Hope you don't mind."

"Course not. I didn't create it myself."

"Well anyway, Shelly kinda turned my head around. Know how? She did a pretend role play in which she was trying to sell me a TV set, but from her point of view and not mine. She was trying to steer me into a particular brand—but only because she was in on a contest to see who could sell how many of it. I was totally turned off. All she talked about was her and the TV. Not me. Said a salesman had used the exact same pitch to her a week ago."

The Agile Manager said nothing.

"You know," continued William, "it's darn hard getting outside of yourself and into someone else's shoes. But that's what you have to do, right?"

"Right."

"Anita, Phil, and I are going to do little brainstorming, then I'll draft *another letter. I'll show it to you tomorrow. Maybe we can turn this failure around."*

The Agile Manager smiled. "Even if you can't, Willie, it sounds like you learned something for next time."

"You bet."

About now you're wondering whether it's time to start writing the first draft yet. Not quite. Writing the draft is the easiest part of your task, so we can put it off for a while yet. There's still one more important consideration: the best arrangement of ideas in the document.

You may consider sequence after writing the draft, of course. Good word-processing software makes cutting and pasting a breeze. But considering sequence up front is better. That will elicit your strongest writing from the start and help you avoid a lot of time-consuming revision.

For example, in starting this book I wrote the last chapter first. I was dealing with several of those last-chapter issues with people who were consulting with me, and so they were topmost on my mind. However, I knew it was to be the last chapter, based on an earlier outline.

You don't have to write in proper sequence. You do, however, need to have a clear idea, before you start, of what the best sequence will be.

This is useful for people who dread that opening sentence or opening paragraph. Avoid the opening until you're ready. Start wherever you feel most comfortable.

Only you know the value of the ideas in your document. Your first job is to convince the reader immediately of that value. One of the best ways to do that is by choosing the best reader-oriented sequence.

SEVEN WAYS TO STRUCTURE A DOCUMENT

Here are schematics for you to use as models for your own projects. I've included the types of documents most appropriate for each.

I'll bet I know the one you've been using until now: I think of it as America's default document. It's almost certainly a variation of our first model, the Main Point Conclusion.

1. The Main Point Conclusion

This is the most familiar mode of American business writing. It tends to be chronological. "Starting at Point X, we did this, we did that, and here are the results with conclusions and recommendations." Diagrammed, it looks like this:

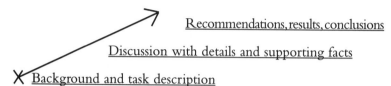

Recommendations, results, conclusions

Discussion with details and supporting facts

Background and task description

May be most useful for:

- Trip reports
- Status reports
- Training reports.

ADVANTAGES:

- Concerned with real time.
- Enables you to "tell a story" to the reader, while showing your thinking step by step.
- Helps the reader to share your conclusion.
- Good way to deliver bad news.

DISADVANTAGES:

- Requires the reader to do a lot of uphill work, slogging along with you every step.
- If the reader is short on time, he/she may discard it or simply skip ahead to your conclusion.
- Most beginners like to show off the time and effort it took to arrive at the conclusion. Readers, however, are not interested.

Plan to Get Action #1

Structuring your documents properly will help to motivate your readers, since your structure is from now on going to be focused on the reader's needs, not the writer's needs. In this and the following four boxes, we'll introduce you to a few action-getting techniques and show you how to use them.

Hit them at the beginning with your best shot. If you were to step into the ring with today's heavyweight boxing champion, what's your best strategy? Come out swinging. Put all your best punches into the first minute because he's not going to give you much time to stay on your feet.

It's true for your business readers as well. They won't give you much time for any kind of pitch, so you might as well give them your best at the start.

Too many writers labor under the fallacy that because they know how valuable the content is, the reader will also sense that value and wait patiently to receive it at the end of a document. The only way to convey value to an indifferent reader is to provide that value up front.

Readers will not give you the luxury of a few paragraphs of warm-up. If you have to write a dozen sentences of warm-up prose to get yourself started, go ahead and do it. Just delete them in the final draft.

It's our old friend background again. Background is to the business writer what cow's milk is to a calf. Most of us seem to think it is indispensable to a proper understanding of what we want the reader to do. In fact, nothing could be further from reality. The past has little value for most business readers—especially your past. They care about today and tomorrow. **To the extent that you talk about the future, to that extent you will succeed.**

There are three good reasons not to craft your documents according to the schematic above:

1. It begins with the past, with old ideas. Many writers like to

begin here because it shows how hard they've been working. Your reader won't care, so avoid this kind of thinking. You can't win with it.

2. It forces readers to (figuratively) work their way uphill, the same way you as the writer had to work uphill to obtain these data. Uphill is not the direction in which most busy people want to go.

3. It delays the latest and most valuable aspect of your document—namely, your recommendations—until the end. Many readers won't make it that far. Of those who do, they are not likely to be at their most receptive and alert, as you have tired them out with lesser information.

It's better to craft your documents with a view to solving all these obstacles right from the start.

2. The Main Point Opening

This is a powerful organizational format. Why? You start from strength, showcasing your best thinking up front, when reader interest is highest. Then you are pulling readers along with you in a rapid, downhill style.

Diagrammed, it looks like this:

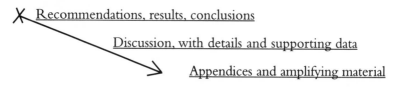

Recommendations, results, conclusions

Discussion, with details and supporting data

Appendices and amplifying material

This is the preferred format for:

- Proposals
- Sales letters
- Customer update letters
- Financial planning
- Memos of all types
- Reports of all types.

ADVANTAGES:

- Readers are helpless to skip to the good stuff, because they're already there.
- The writer is firmly in control.
- Follows the natural tendencies of people to have a short attention span.
- Delivers the most important message up front.

DISADVANTAGES:

- May be a shock to the reader, who was expecting something more traditional.
- Forces the reader to skip around in time.
- Demands sophistication of the reader.

Here's an example adapted from an actual case study. For purposes of discussion, let's say our hero company, Bulldog Mowers, is an international maker of commercial riding mowers, the kind you see grooming golf courses and cemeteries.

The writer, in Bulldog's marketing department, is sending this report throughout the organization.

Competitor plant tours are routine among all major players in the industry. This is not industrial espionage. The writer wants Bulldog personnel to come back with useful intelligence.

Let's begin with the Planning Guide:

Planning Guide

1. The main reason I am writing this is to alert all personnel who visit competing factories to focus on our competitors' thinking rather than hardware.

2. The problem the reader has that I can solve is he/she doesn't know the most useful observations to make during competitive plant tours.

3. The actions I want the reader to take are (a) to plan competitive plant tours intelligently, possibly by writing down questions and strategies ahead of time and (b) tuck this away in a briefcase and use it as a guide for taking notes and writing up trip reports on all future visits.

Plan to Get Action #2

Write your text as long as necessary, staying concise and well formatted. To motivate readers, long text beats short text every time. This is one of the universal tenets of direct mail. Use this principle to advantage when trying to get readers to respond or perform some specific action, such as calling you or filling out a business reply card.

If, for example, you are offering your readers a free seminar on a professional topic of interest to them, don't think that a short description of the seminar, plus dates and places, will generate action. It likely will not. Why? Because any request for a large block of the reader's time isn't free. Your readers are paying for it with lost time and lost work. They understand that instinctively.

Your invitation should come with a multi-page discussion of what's in it for them to attend in the first place. While your cover letter may be short, your reasons for attending should be compelling and complete.

Many organizations seem to be caught in the "One Page Only" trap. To motivate readers to action, take as many pages as necessary, but make those pages reader-friendly and concise.

Can you be concise and yet write lengthy documents at the same time? Yes. Concise writing uses just enough of the right words to convey meaning accurately. Length is a function of the complexity of your message. A 200-page proposal can—and should—be concise.

4. My most important reader-centered idea is <u>to focus future plant visits on management systems.</u>

5. The reader's two most-critical professional concerns are <u>(a) appearing competent in the eyes of competitors and (b) making the tour of sufficient value to justify the expense.</u>

6. The reader's likely reaction to my ideas will be <u>NEUTRAL</u>.

(If the reader is likely to be neutral or positive, my main idea goes at the beginning. If the reader is likely to be negative, my main idea goes after a brief warm-up.)

Now that we have a solid idea of what this document is about, let's consider the arrangement of ideas. The one that follows is, I believe, fresh and arresting. It may serve as a useful model for your own projects.

COMPETITIVE PLANT VISITS: A MEANS TO IMPROVE BULLDOG MOWERS MANUFACTURING IN A GLOBAL MARKETPLACE

Conclusions

1. This year, Sunrise Mowers of Taiwan (SMT) seems to be gearing up to produce a world-dominating riding mower to coincide with the 2004 Industrial Mower Manufacturers' Conference.

2. SMT's plant operations are not nearly as efficient as France's Toujour Mowers. SMT is making serious efforts but has a long way to go.

This general summary of SMT's manufacturing and assembly capabilities suggests how Bulldog can learn from Taiwan's mistakes.

Recommendation: Focus future plant visits on management systems.

Bulldog people who visit SMT and Toujour plants should focus on the "why" of what the plants are doing and proposing, rather than on hardware and physical layout. To do this, ask strategic questions about:
* Management styles
* Engineering
* Human resources practices, policies, and procedures.

Monsoon Bay Plant is the key to SMT's plans

SMT began a modernization project for its Monsoon Bay Plant two years ago. Completion date: 27 months.

Their heavy investment in this plant suggests plans for a world-class triple-deck riding mower that could be a serious competitor for Bulldog, the industry leader for 21 years.

Action requested

Try to see the Monsoon Bay plant before agreeing to tour any
other of SMT's operations.

SMT'S STRATEGIC STRENGTHS

SMT emulates Japanese workforce techniques

It seems to be trying to achieve Japanese-style work practices with training work teams and other techniques. History shows this to be essential if any company is to compete successfully with the Japanese. Such efforts demonstrate SMT's commitment.

SMT mirrors Swiss engineering

The company is in step with contemporary manufacturing strategies. It appears to be following the Swiss engineering style of achieving a clear advantage through internal machine tool
* design
* development
* installation.

SMT hires only technically proficient employees

SMT is in step with current worldwide mower-deck design using the latest CAD advances. Over time, this will give it a highly flexible workforce.

Important note

Halfway through this tour I realized that SMT's strengths lay in
such things as teamwork and engineering practices. Had I been
focused strictly on machinery, plant layout, and the like—as I am
on most plant tours—I would have missed the personnel innovations that SMT has put into practice. If you go, I hope you will see
this for yourself and provide us with a richer investigation.

SMT'S STRATEGIC WEAKNESSES

Process may be out of control or not capable

A recent Bulldog white paper on SMT suggests (page 108) a need for extensive body repair after build. Conclusion: This problem may be too expensive to solve.

Paint quality depends on air-scrubber effectiveness

The foundry and paint shop are on the same site. While facilities and systems prevent airborne grit from entering the paint shop, any reduction in performance will almost surely result in paint degradation.

Foundry product strategy is ill-defined

The white paper mentions the manufacture of ventilated disc brakes, drums, blocks, and camshafts totaling 50 tons per day. This is hard to understand since the machining center on the same site makes axles.

Robotics raises questions

* SMT installed 91 Juta robots in the Monsoon Bay body shop. Korea makes Juta robots, not known for reliability. SMT's use of them suggests a connection unknown before now and a potential source of financial support.
* In critical areas, such as deck-plate and blade installation, SMT bought Japanese-made Kudo robots.

(Note: most of the information in this report comes from SMT brochures, three visit reports, and a Bulldog of Europe white paper.)

Please notice the strengths of this document design:

- Conclusions and recommendations are right up front.
- Reader understands what writer is requesting immediately.
- Uses an eye-pleasing column format for easy reading and easy comprehension of complex information.
- Entire format uses most-important to least-important arrangement, meaning readers can drop off at any point beyond the first page and still have all the vital information.
- Takes advantage of a fresh look on the page to intrigue readers who might not necessarily be lured in by the subject.

3. Inverted Pyramid

This is a variation of the main point beginning. It is the sole organization style of most big-league newspaper stories. Principle: Pack all of the information at the beginning, because the reader will not stay with you for the entire piece.

Diagrammed, it looks like this:

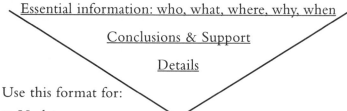

Essential information: who, what, where, why, when

Conclusions & Support

Details

Use this format for:

- Updates
- Status reports
- Customer newsletters
- Internal memos.

ADVANTAGES:	DISADVANTAGES:
■ Assumes the reader is not going to read every word.	■ Tends to be fact-based and terse, allowing little room for personality.
■ Keeps writer in control.	
■ Enhances editing if project becomes too lengthy.	■ May not be preferred by a people-oriented supervisor.

4. *Descending Importance*

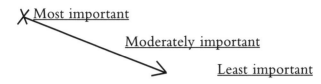

Most important

Moderately important

Least important

Use this schematic to organize your ideas for:

- Business letters
- Sales letters
- Status reports
- Meeting minutes
- Trip reports where the value of a sales call or activity is more important than the sequence in which it occurred.

Plan to Get Action #3

Use lots of subheads, captions, and a postscript. Copy testing over several decades underscores another writing secret that you can take to the bank.

There are three elements in every good letter that human beings are helpless to avoid:

- Headlines
- Captions
- Postscripts.

A good headline captures attention and drives the reader to find out more.

Captions under charts or photographs are irresistible. You should always write captions that contain solid nuggets of persuasion.

Postscripts have about them, I believe, an air of gossip, and thus are equally irresistible. Some people feel a postscript is inappropriate in a business letter. However, knowing how powerfully they attract readership, how can you not use them?

Repeat in different words your best offer in a postscript. If possible, put in a time-limited benefit or bonus that readers will receive if they respond before such-and-such a date.

ADVANTAGES:
- Breaks out of the chronological mold.
- Enables writer to deal with importance versus actual occurrence.
- Enhances editing if project becomes too lengthy.

DISADVANTAGES:
- Tends to confuse people who expect literal adherence to a time line.
- Takes the most time to reorganize and rewrite.

5. *Time-Line Working Forward*

Earliest

Mid-range

Most recent

Use this schematic to organize your ideas for:

- Laboratory reports where the process is most important
- Trip reports where every sales call or activity is of equal importance
- Progress reports where maintaining a schedule is important
- Meeting minutes where the legal department requires a chronological record.

Tip: Even where reporting issues in the right time sequence is valuable, put a summary at the top highlighting the most important ideas within the document.

ADVANTAGES:
- Mirrors events as they actually happened.
- Keeps writer in control.
- Enhances editing if project becomes too lengthy.

DISADVANTAGES:
- Makes all events seem equally important, even if they weren't.
- Tends to be boring in a lengthy format.

Plan to Get Action #4

Sell the offer, not the product. This is another time-tested principle of direct selling. It's much easier, in written communications, to persuade the reader to come to a free seminar (to continue our earlier example) than to buy a $250,000 software program.

The offer is an efficient way for you to establish a human connection with your audience.

It allows the reader to test out the main claims you're making for your product or service. For example, if you're selling software that totally enhances the way a salesperson on the road communicates with the home office, your offer might be a free booklet on "Using Laptops to Make the Tough Sell."

It's also a good idea to tell the reader right up front that you're not asking for any money. Instead, offer a free sample, or a free ten-minute consultation, or whatever a reasonable offer is for you.

It's relatively easy to sell people on trying something on a small scale, rather than move them immediately into the big purchase.

That's why (to use an example from common experience) a car salesperson first tries to talk a customer into a free test drive. That's easy! Once he/she has established rapport, a basis for personal trust, then it's time for the big sell.

6. Time-Line Working Backward

Use this schematic to organize your ideas for:

- Laboratory reports where the data, conclusions, or recommendations are most important.
- Trip reports where the value of a sales call or activity is

---

Plan to Get Action #5

Get them to like you. This may sound odd but it's absolutely true. People do business with people they like. When you think about it, you'll believe me, because that's how you are, too.

In terms of writing, getting them to like you means letting some personality shine through. Tell examples. Reveal some of your personal background. Don't be afraid of gentle humor, especially to show your own human foibles. Be brisk and businesslike, of course, but be human too, just as you would in face-to-face communication.

---

more important than the actual calendar sequence in which it occurred.

- Status reports where maintaining a schedule is crucial.

ADVANTAGE:	DISADVANTAGE:
■ Enables writer to emphasize current issues.	■ Difficult to follow.

7. *The Classic Outline: An Example*

A report on upgrading home-office computers.

I. Overview
   A. History of computer purchases
   B. Falling behind competitors
   C. Obstacles to purchase
II. Experiences of others in our industry
   A. Wow Tech, Inc.
   B. Star Tech, Inc.
      1. Failure to upgrade
      2. Response of marketplace
      3. Loss of market share
III. Costs
   A. Financing
   B. Personnel
   C. Training

IV. Long-range plans

V. Recommendation

Use this schematic to organize your ideas for:

- Proposals
- Process descriptions
- Status reports
- Lengthy documents where maintaining continuity is crucial
- Professional articles
- Situation analyses.

ADVANTAGES:	DISADVANTAGES:
• Traditional, logical. • Familiar to readers.	• Predictable, potentially boring. • Unless subject is compelling or a rigid order is crucial, lack of originality may mean you forfeit readership.

In some instances, Method 1 or Method 7 may be the best way to structure a document. But those should be quite rare. Please do not use them as default structures the way most business writers do today. Instead, let your knowledge of the reader's needs and interests guide your selection of a method that will be more strategic and more effective.

The Agile Manager's Checklist

✔ Know the seven ways to structure the document you're writing. There's a time and a place to use each.

✔ Remember, however, to use caution when using the Main Point Conclusion or the Classic Outline. When you use either, there's a good chance you'll lose the reader.

✔ When in doubt, employ the Main Point Opening. It's your best bet to incite the reader to action.

Chapter Four

Now Let's Write The First Draft

The Agile Manager steeled himself as he began to read the draft of William's letter. "Dear Ms. Halsey," it began. "You've built a beautiful worldwide marketing pipeline, and it's filled with useful products. But as you know, you must keep shoveling products into the pipeline to keep your customers happy. I believe we can jointly design and produce products that will enhance your reputation for quality and boost your sales. And we can do it in a way that improves your bottom line."

The Agile Manager relaxed his shoulders. Not perfect, he thought, but 180 degrees from the first one. He continued to read, hoping to find a direct request. He found it at the bottom of the second page: "I've worked up some designs I think your medical technology group could sell through its Health-for-All retail outlets. I also worked up a few bare-bones cost estimates that show these designs have the potential to exceed your average return on investment in this area. May I have twenty minutes of your time next week to drop them off and explain them? I'll call your assistant on Monday to see if we can arrange a time."

Fantastic, thought the Agile Manager as he went over the letter again, marveling at its tone and the way he consistently discussed financial benefits to her throughout. Where'd Willie pick that up? He wouldn't know a debit from a credit, let alone a return ratio. I just have to make sure he knows what it means if he gets in to see her. Which is still doubtful . . .

Theories abound about writing the first draft of any document. Some successful business writers polish as they write. Others amass research while letting the pressure of a deadline build, then dash off a first draft in a white heat of creativity.

If you are typical of the great majority, you have to balance writing hard-working documents within the normal pressures of a business day. Here's what I recommend:

Think of the first draft the way a sculptor thinks of that large lump of clay. Getting it from an amorphous blob to a recognizable shape is all you're trying to do.

The first draft, then, is where you combine all your important ideas within an optimal arrangement. It's a starting point. If you think of it merely as the first step, you will take away most of the fear associated with writing and be able to concentrate on the quality of your ideas.

Don't agonize over writing. Just sit down and write! You can analyze to your heart's content later.

Here are two sayings all writers would be wise to keep in mind:

- *Don't get it right—get it written.*
- *Writing is rewriting.*

Example: I am writing this paragraph during the first draft. I feel little pressure to make this paragraph or the entire draft flawless for three reasons.

First, the deadline is comfortably over the horizon. As a professional, like you, I do not procrastinate while waiting for inspiration to strike. Inspiration does not strike. It waits to make sure you're willing to work, then helps you over the rough spots.

Second, I did not wait until I had a great opening. At this point, I'm still not sure what my opening is going to be. I simply wrote an outline, then started in on a section for which I had the keenest interest.

Third, I am allowing myself time for at least two revisions before submitting this to the editor. Revising is where good writing happens. It, too, takes place in a state of relative tranquillity because you have the peace of mind in knowing you're working from a complete draft—the hard part will be over.

I have been through this stage many times before, and I know it is where I will catch most of my mistakes and poor constructions. This knowledge keeps me relaxed during the writing of the first draft. The first draft will be far from perfect. What's most important is that the ideas are strong to begin with.

Use Pressure to Help Keep You Going

Deadlines are a fact of a writer's life. Most of your writing projects will occur under the pressure of time. This is for the most part a good thing, as it forces even the perfectionists among us to get it done as best they can and ship it out.

Often you labor under the pressure of someone who has to approve your writing while not necessarily being sympathetic to it. This is also a fact of a writer's life. More often than not, I write for people's approval who have never met me or know me only superficially. It's another source of pressure—one that I do my best to reduce by asking for a face-to-face meeting whenever possible.

I'm not saying you can avoid pressure. Far from it. What you can avoid is the panic that comes from not knowing what to do next, or not knowing the best process in the first place. You have enough tools and enough process in this book so that from now on you'll know what to do next. You'll know how to come up with ideas that seem so hard to nail down.

Good Pressure Versus Bad Pressure

Good pressure is energizing. Having a reasonable deadline up ahead, knowing you're capable of seeing the project through, understanding the essential process of building on a solid foundation—that's all good pressure. It's like being a talented athlete, trained and in shape, adrenaline pumping, ready for the event. That's when you can use pressure to bring out your best performance.

Best Tip

Write under a deadline—even if you have to set it yourself. It'll help you tame that monster called procrastination.

Bad pressure saps your energies and makes you feel helpless. Working under unreasonable restrictions, writing for someone who tends to treat your work lightly, knowing that people have failed to agree up front or will use your work for political purposes—that's all bad pressure.

Get everyone involved. I find the best way to defuse this bad pressure is to call a meeting of everyone involved. Pass out blank copies of the Planning Guide. Fill in the answers together. Insist on agreement. When you do this properly, everyone will have some stake in the outcome. Obtaining approval will be much easier.

Practical Steps for a Successful Outcome

Plan to take the maximum time allowed, and avoid distractions.

Let's say, for example, your supervisor asks you to deliver a status report in two working days. You agree that delivery is possible. The first step is to decide how much actual writing time you have, given that the daily workload doesn't go away. With a realistic number of hours in your head, do this:

1. Fill out the Planning Guide.
2. Spend thirty minutes in an idea-generating exercise such as questioning, mindmapping, or brainstorming. If possible,

enlist a handful of colleagues to help with brainstorming.

3. Put all the important ideas on separate index cards.

4. Consider the best reader-oriented arrangement of those ideas. Begin with one of the formats I suggest in chapter three. Move the index cards around until you get an effective flow of ideas.

Plan to use up a full 30 percent of your allotted writing time to get to this point.

5. Turn on your computer and start writing, your index cards in front of you as a guide. Ignore any impulse to correct, change, or rewrite. Just concentrate on getting all of your ideas written.

Use 40 percent of your allotted time writing the first draft.

6. Take a break. Work on another project. Make phone calls. If the deadline allows, sleep on it. You'll find that getting distance from the project allows your mind to ease away from pride of authorship.

    With distance, you can approach the project more objectively, as if someone else had written it. You'll find more errors that way, and you'll be more willing to delete some of those expressions you fell in love with in the first draft that now seem inappropriate in a formal draft.

7. Now go back and revise until your time is up.

You should allow the remaining 30 percent of your allotted time for revising.

Start Writing from Strength

In chapter two, I recommended some tools for capturing good ideas:

- Brainstorming and mindmapping
- Questioning
- Index cards
- Research.

Using most or all of these techniques will prepare you for the challenge of writing an effective document. Once you have your ideas arranged on index cards, the document has a skeleton, a definite shape. You're over a big hurdle! You should feel good about the status of your project to this point; your mind should feel relaxed.

These tools will also help you draw a clear mental picture of your reader—your prospect. They will enable you to visualize the specific physical actions you want your reader to do.

In other words, you are as well prepared to write as you are ever going to be. Remember the sage advice of Mary Poppins: "Well begun is nearly done."

Go After That Elusive Reader

Professional writers use certain powerful techniques to intrigue readers and lure them into the text. The trick is to make it easy for readers to find your key ideas and absorb your message. Here's how you do it:

The Ten-Best Writing Techniques

1. Use subheads—your most powerful tool—as idea guides.
2. Attract interest immediately with your most strategic idea first.
3. Stay in your reader's shoes through the first draft.
4. Write tight, concise prose.
5. Keep your vocabulary plain and unadorned.
6. Use short sentences and short paragraphs.
7. Pull the reader along with action verbs and active voice.
8. Streamline your prose to make the power of your ideas stand out.
9. Use the style and tone appropriate for the occasion.
10. Be positive all the time.

Let's discuss these techniques one at a time.

1. Use Subheads as Idea Guides

Subheads have been the great unsung heroes of the writer's

art since the beginning of mass communication. As a means of directing the reader's attention from one idea to the next, they are indispensable. Magazine and newspaper writers use them unstintingly. Direct-mail specialists would fold up their laptops and go home if ever denied them. (Check out the next piece of direct mail that comes across your desk and you'll see what I mean.)

Best Tip

Use 30 percent of your time to gather ideas, 40 percent to write the first draft, and 30 percent to revise your work.

You, as a professional business writer, should use subheads in everything you write, from simple memos and meeting minutes to lengthy proposals. I believe you should use whatever works, consistent with your image. Subheads are the hardest working, most dependable tool you will ever come across.

I offered this counsel recently to a group of twenty-five senior vice presidents at one of America's most prestigious and forward-thinking companies. They listened to me politely, then began throwing bricks at my arguments.

"We don't want to come off like some slick advertising types."

"Our company is too traditional."

"Subheads are okay for junk mail, but my documents are not junk."

This went on for some minutes until one of the younger participants raised his hand for a comment.

The best argument for subheads I've ever heard. "Let me tell you all what happened to me," he said, "just last week. I'm still stunned by it."

Having won the room's attention, he said that he was sitting in his supervisor's outer office one morning, waiting for an appointment. The administrative assistant, he noticed, was opening the interoffice mail. She happened to take out of the envelope a document he himself had sent the previous day.

"I was really interested to see how the process worked," he said. "And I found out."

The assistant gave his document a quick scan and then—wonder of wonders!—she reached across her desk and picked up a yellow highlighter marker.

"She proceeded," he said, "to highlight the passages in the document she felt the boss would be most interested in. I sat there with my mouth open. I had no idea it worked like that!"

There was silence in the room while everyone thought about that story.

"Tell us more about using subheads," someone said. I did. They took notes.

Who will highlight your ideas? This issue is important. Someone, at some point along the communications path, is going to highlight for your primary reader what he or she thinks that person should read. Since you are the writer, I believe you are best qualified to determine what the important points are. You should do the highlighting.

Use subheads to highlight ideas and show the document's structure.

What's the best way to highlight the important ideas? With subheads.

In the example that starts on the following page, notice how hard subheads work to:

- Convey the most important ideas
- Give your document a clear structure
- Offer readers the option of not necessarily reading every paragraph
- Indicate urgency by using verbs
- Clarify your message.

This example is a press release to magazine editors concerning a new business venture:

May 28, 20XX

Editor John Smith
Tech Charge Magazine
1234 Main Street
Middletown, OH 01234

Subj: Making a new impact on the Internet

Dear Mr. Smith:

Your readers will surely enjoy a timely story about
how our new joint venture provides an overdue
example of how to approach Web design.

With the urgency to get a presence on the Web, even
the most savvy businesses neglect a fundamental
marketing strategy. With few alternatives, they put
their trust in computer specialists whose background
is not marketing or advertising. Or in an advertising
agency whose expertise does not include electronic
media development.

A pioneering approach merges two areas of expertise

HMC~Signal.com takes a distinctively different
approach to marketing on the web. The company is a
joint venture between Harwood Moses Chambers
Advertising and Signal Advertising. HMC brings the
resources of a full-service advertising agency to this
venture. Signal provides the technological and engineering expertise in Web site design, promotion, and
management.

We begin by assessing the business

HMC~Signal.com begins in the right place—with an
assessment of a client's business, competitors' sites,
and a strategic plan that integrates site design with
marketing goals.

This new venture offers the blending of marketing professionals, creative teams, and computer/software engineers to meet all the criteria needed to communicate effectively in the digital marketplace.

<u>You'll find details in our press pack</u>

It includes art from our new Web site and the sites of some of our clients (disk and hard copies), and more about **HMC~Signal.com**—the people, the services, and the clients. Please feel free to contact any of our clients for quotes.

<u>Next step</u>

I'll call you soon to get your response.

Sincerely,

K. C. Cronin
Public Relations Director
[Reprinted with permission of the author]

Some writers like to boldface their subheads. Others put them in all capitals or all italics. For letters and other everyday projects, I prefer them underlined, in the same typeface as the rest of your document.

2. *Attract Interest Immediately with Your Most Strategic Idea First*

Hitting readers with your strongest idea first will do more than grab their attention. It will astonish them.

Few people write in such an effective way today. Most are stuck in the old "background first" rut and will never change. By taking a different—more strategic—approach, you will convey an additional subliminal message that your thinking is fresh and to the point.

Even better, you will ensure that readers will get your most important idea, even if they get nothing else.

3. Stay in Your Reader's Shoes through the First Draft

Writing from another's point of view is difficult. It takes imagination and constant self-reminding. It pays off, however, in response. People notice whether you are talking about them and their needs or about yourself and your goals.

Writing from the reader's perspective is a powerful technique. It liberates you. It narrows your topics to a few, but those few will work because the reader has an inherent interest in them.

One good way to develop the *You* attitude as a writing habit is to begin your opening paragraph with "You." It is a can't-miss reminder that what interests the reader might be far different from what interests the writer. You need the reader's interest if you are going to be successful.

Remember: "I might be selling grass seed, but my customer is buying a beautiful lawn."

4. Write Tight, Concise Prose

For almost a century, *The Kansas City Star* was one of America's premier daily newspapers. Readers universally admired it for clean, uncluttered prose that told the story without making the reader wade through a field of adverbs and adjectives.

Just after World War I, a young man fresh from his duties as an ambulance driver in Europe applied for a cub reporter's job. The city editor saw some promise and hired him, giving him the paper's style sheet as a guide. Here it is, reprinted in its entirety.

The Kansas City Star Style Sheet
1. Use short sentences.
2. Use short first paragraphs.
3. Use vigorous English.
4. Be positive, not negative.

The young reporter, Ernest Hemingway, thought this was sound advice. He later built a career as a novelist on it.

The "one-page" mis-rule. People in workshops are constantly telling me that their supervisors have imposed a "one-page rule" on all documents. Nothing can be longer than one page.

I think this is misguided. What the supervisors are really after with that rule is concise, effective writing. They feel that by forcing writers to one page maximum, they will get short, strong prose.

What they actually get, unfortunately, is undeveloped, half-baked writing with not nearly the amount or quality of ideas it takes to make the sale or move the project ahead.

Remember the direct mail rule of thumb: If you want a response (and who doesn't?), a long document works better than a short one.

What I mean by long text is a you-oriented document that uses

—short words

—short sentences

—short paragraphs

structured around verb-based subheads. The subheads showcase the main ideas, while the prose is lean and forceful. That kind of quality writing can go on for dozens of pages and be far more effective than one page of stilted, cliché-ridden prose.

5. Keep Your Vocabulary Plain and Unadorned

Coaches tell athletes to "stay within your game." They mean don't take foolish chances. Play to your strengths. Don't swing for home runs if you're gifted at punching the ball to the opposite field for singles. Keep your first serve in play, even if it means taking off some speed.

It's the same for writers. Use only words you know to be correct. Look up any words you're unsure about.

For instance, "sanguine" and "sanguinary" are polar opposites. Do you know the difference? Learning how you could misapply them is a good lesson in being careful about word choice.

Or take a deceptively easy word such as "sanction." Its first two primary meanings are exact opposites. Are you sure your reader is going to know which meaning you have in mind?

Another example. Do you know how many definitions exist for the word "frog"? The word can hardly be simpler. One would think little confusion would arise by using it. Yet there are over forty different ways to understand the word. Among its many other different definitions, "frog" can mean:

- The bridge under the strings of a violin
- A derogatory slang term for a person of French origin
- A button on a heavy wool coat
- Or, oh yes, that little green amphibian.

If you use "frog" in a document, be sure your reader knows which of those forty-plus definitions you mean. The more complex your word choice, the more careful you have to be that you and your reader share the same definition.

Staying within your game also includes being careful about foreign terms. With so much international business being conducted these days, this is crucial.

Maybe "Heir" means "bonehead" in German. I was consulting with "Jack," an American engineer in an international manufacturing company. He showed me several documents he was working on in collaboration with his counterpart in Germany, also an engineer.

Always, always, always write from the reader's perspective. To keep yourself focused, use 'you' instead of 'I.'

Included was a letter to this colleague that began:

"Dear Heir Muller . . ."

I pointed to the salutation and asked him what "Heir" meant.

"That's the German word for 'Mister,'" the engineer said.

"Are you sure?" I said.

"Oh yes, it is," he said. He was getting impatient with me. He wanted to move on to more important matters. We both looked at the word some more. I was trying to think how best to break the bad news to him.

"It means *mister* in German," he repeated. "I should know, I've been writing to this guy for five years."

I went over to the blackboard. "Jack," I said, "I minored in German in college. This—" (I wrote *Herr* on the blackboard) "—is the German word for Mister."

When in doubt, use short, Anglo-Saxon words instead of multisyllabic Latin-based words (like *die* instead of *expire*).

He looked at *Herr* for a moment, and then realized to his horror that I was right. What happened next was something I'd read about but never seen before. The blood drained from his face. I was afraid he would faint.

Why such a strong reaction? He realized that making a mistake with something so easy to check, like the German word for "mister," rendered his conclusions, his research, his recommendations all suspect to poor Herr Muller.

Play within your game. Use words you know or are willing to look up. A good rule of thumb: choose Anglo-Saxon based words over Latin-based words whenever possible. Any good dictionary will tell you what a word's origin is. If you can, select those that come from Old English or Middle English. It's better, for example, to choose

lie (Old English) over *prevaricate* (Latin)
best (Middle English) over *optimum* (L)
end (OE) over *abrogate* (L)
think (OE) over *cogitate* (L).

Anglo-Saxon based words tend to be easier to define and understand. They have fewer alternate shades of meaning. They have the virtue of plainness. Plain speaking and plain writing suggest an ability to get to the heart of a matter—an ability you want others to see in you.

There's an even thornier issue here. In choosing simpler words over more complex ones, will your readers think you are ill-educated or lacking in intelligence? I think not.

First, your readers, if they don't know you, will likely not think anything one way or the other. They're too busy, remember, thinking about their own concerns.

Second, almost no one will study your document. They'll scan it, looking for the important parts. The clearer and simpler you are, the more likely they are to get your message.

Third, your agenda is to communicate ideas, not to impress with your vocabulary.

Other writers may have different agendas. Political commentators such as William F. Buckley and George Will, on the other hand, are trying to impress readers with the scope of their erudition and breadth of learning. If they are clearly smarter than anyone else, they are not as apt to have to endure rebuttals from readers. That's why they use obscure (but delicious) Latinate words all the time.

College professors, too, consider it their duty to use every multi-syllabic word at their command. They would consider it part of what you're paying for when you read their books or attend their classes.

Often, such writers are correct. Complex ideas deserve complex vocabulary. Scholars employ grand concepts such as objective correlative and deconstruction sometimes because those are the only words available to carry us to the frontiers of philosophy.

You and I, however, are mostly writing about products and services to a wide audience, from Harvard MBAs to people who speak English as a second language.

Keep it simple. Your readers will respond by giving you their business. Save your impressive vocabulary for the next alumni reunion.

6. Use Short Sentences and Short Paragraphs

In their excellent book *Fit for Life*, Harvey and Marilyn Diamond suggest a profound concept about the uses and misuses of energy. Digestion, they point out, takes by far the greatest amount of energy from our bodies. No other activity—running, lifting weights, pole vaulting—even comes close. Our bodies labor mightily to digest the food we so cavalierly put into them.

That explains why we fall asleep in the afternoons after a big lunch. The energy that should go into keeping us awake and productive has to go toward digestion.

The same principle applies to writing. If readers have to devote any of the precious energy they've decided to give to your document in "digesting" huge words and bulky sentences and fat paragraphs, they will feel a similar drop in attention and have that much less energy to devote to your ideas.

Best Tip

If you're using a word from a foreign language, make certain you know what it means and that you're spelling it right.

By the way, the sentence above is forty-six words—three times the ideal length of fifteen words. As a reader, you have to devote some energy towards keeping all of those separate ideas in the air until you reach the period. See if this is better:

> Help readers to conserve precious mental energy. Huge words, bulky sentences, and fat paragraphs require extra digestive vigor. They decrease attention. Whatever energy readers waste, they won't have to devote to your ideas.

Isn't that easier? Can you feel your cognitive power staying high through four short sentences? And dissipating through one long one? Your readers will experience the same thing.

Short words, short sentences, short paragraphs all save reading energy—energy you want prospects and customers to devote to understanding your pitch and responding to your offer.

7. *Pull the Reader Along with Action Verbs and Active Voice*

The great majority of business documents I see during a normal working day and in writing workshops feature go-nowhere verbs and lazy passive expressions. Most people seem to think this is accepted business style. They don't want to be seen as too aggressive or too pushy.

Consequently, their documents are so bland they don't even register on a reader's Richter Scale and end up floating lazily into the recycling bin.

Best Tip

Use the active voice. Say, "I hope that we'll succeed," instead of, "Success is greatly hoped for."

Too many writers expect readers to do at least some of the work. That's why there is so much fat, lazy writing for an average business reader to wade through on any given day.

Smart writers, in contrast, know that readers are unwilling to do any work at all. They write strong, lean prose that always stands out. It's so unusual to get a clear, forcefully written document that readers can't help but pay attention when they see it.

The best evidence that your writing is strong and lean is the active voice. Voice denotes the person or thing involved in the action. In the active voice, the person or entity performing the action is in front of the verb—pushing the action. In the passive voice, that person or entity is behind the verb—pulling the action. Here are some examples:

Active voice: The management team *planned* the program.
Passive voice: The program *was planned* by the management team.

Active voice: Wendy Fairfax *will win* the Kiwanis scholarship.
Passive voice: The Kiwanis scholarship *will be won* by Wendy Fairfax.

Active voice: The building and grounds department *is issuing* a new set of regulations for employee parking.
Passive voice: A new set of regulations for employee parking *is being issued* by the building and grounds department.

Both active and passive voices are grammatically correct. However, can you see how active voice improves the writing?

Active voice is:

- Stronger
- More direct
- More pleasant to read
- More descriptive of what is actually happening
- Shorter.

Passive voice is:

- Weaker
- Indirect
- Longer.

Passive voice generally uses some form of the verb *to be*, making it by definition longer than active voice.

Passive voice has its place. Legal prose uses it almost exclusively, because its primary virtue is to avoid direct responsibility. Scientists tend to prefer passive voice as well, thinking that experiments and data should stand on their own, rather than be the result of some specific person doing the action.

For most business purposes, however, active is the voice of choice. Use it to keep your writing lean and sharp.

8. Streamline Your Prose to Make the Power of Your Ideas Stand Out

An industrial designer coined the word "streamline" in the 1920s. Pan American Airlines had hired him to transform its aircraft from freight carriers to passenger carriers. The idea was to improve efficiency through the air to make the transformation cost-effective.

"Streamline" is a useful term to describe any improvement in design that cuts down air resistance and enhances performance. It's just as powerful an idea for writers as for aircraft designers. Think of it also as clearing out dead wood or cutting out the fat.

See if this visual example helps. Using too many words in your writing is like brewing your coffee with too much water. It becomes so tasteless you won't be able to drink even the most expensive coffee. Similarly, too many words weaken your writing, making even the best ideas seem soggy and valueless. Readers will quickly tire and stop reading.

Strong fresh writing, like strong fresh coffee, quickens the blood, and makes the reader want more. Here's how to do it:

   a. Eliminate words that don't drive the action forward.

      Enclosed please find . . .

      It goes without saying that . . .

      As I said before . . .

      It is to be hoped that . . .

      Please be advised . . .

   b. Eliminate words that try to amplify or enhance but miss the mark.

      very

      really

      truly

      quite

   c. Eliminate windbag words that try to be sophisticated but fail.

      utilize

      in the event that

      indicate

      advise

   d. Eliminate jargon, in-group vocabulary, abbreviations, or any other unusual expressions that hinder rather than add to the understanding.

      FYI, I need a CYA memo for the files ASAP.

9. Use the Style and Tone Appropriate for the Occasion.

Is the style right? Style is your personality on paper. You choose a certain writing style for the same reason you choose a certain set of clothing—for the effect. Choosing the wrong style or tone could have the wrong effect.

Just as you don't go to an embassy dinner in jeans and sport coat, you don't write a formal report in casual prose. You formalize your writing for formal occasions, and tone it down for more casual projects, including e-mail. Your writing style should be as adaptable as your clothing style.

Use a consistent style to characterize your own writing. Lots of people, for example, could tell by looking at a few paragraphs of prose whether Hemingway wrote it—his style is that distinctive. Picasso's paintings have a style that differs from Leonardo daVinci's. It's relatively easy to tell J. S. Bach's music from Mozart's.

Style is an extension of the personality you choose to convey. For most general business writing, a fifty-fifty combination of personable and professional will get the job done.

Best Tip

Vary your tone depending on the occasion. You don't want to sound the same in writing a congratulatory note as you would in writing a warning.

Good writing is active and personal. Weak writing has words that slow the reader down, is too passive, and is so dry you can hardly believe a real person had anything to do with it.

Here's an example of what I mean. "It is felt by the management team that in order to remain in a competitive posture vis-à-vis new product development and for testing of various univariate relationships, planning must be accomplished for an expansion of research facilities in a narrow time frame."

I think the writer is saying let's expand the lab now while we're competitive, but I'm not sure. Neither, I suspect, is the writer.

The example is wordy, passive, and devoid of personality—of enthusiasm for the work. You have to read it twice to get any idea of what the reader wants.

Is your tone right? Tone is a variation of style to suit the particular situation.

Let's say you need to write a letter sharply rebuking a vendor for delivering a poor-quality product or service. Your overall style is genuine and professional—you never abandon that personable/professional attitude that serves as your hallmark as a business writer. However, your tone for this one letter should be strong enough to make the reader understand your displeasure.

Another case: You wish to commend someone in your group for a job well done. Your style even here is personable/professional. Now, however, you tilt slightly in the direction of personable.

Tone is how you convey professionally your attitude of the moment. Here's a good example of how one manager used concise prose and an appropriate style and tone to pick up sales:

MEMO

October 22, 20XX

From: Stephanie Crane, VP Accounts Manager
To: New New-Business Team
Subj: New Accounts — where to find 'em, how to wow 'em

<u>"We're here to chew bubble gum and kick butt. And we're all out of bubble gum."</u>

That's what a football player said before a game last week on national TV. And that's the attitude toward new business I want us to have companywide.

<u>New-business team sets the tone</u>

You and I are responsible for a lot more than new business. We're the front edge, so we're what everybody else in the organization looks to for leadership and definition. For too long we've been simply minding the store. For too long, we've let accounts come to us.

From now on, we're hunters.

<u>First task: pick our targets</u>

Please come to the next meeting with the contact names for five fat, juicy, up-for-grabs accounts that we've

---

never gone after before. Criteria:
* gross sales above $25 million
* employee base of at least 100
* industries with which we have some history, especially travel and automotive
* based within 1,000 miles of our main office (2-3 air hours).

Important: please collate names with other team members before the meeting to avoid duplication.

<u>Second task: create single effective marketing tool</u>
Let's brainstorm during next session. Front-runner possibilities include (in order of probability):
1. New brochure
2. Revised web site
3. CD-ROM
4. New prospect-oriented video.

<u>Action requested</u>

Please meet with me next Wednesday for a two-hour session. Bring ideas and lunch.

Third-floor conference room, noon to two p.m.

Some features to notice about this hard-working memo. First, it borders on informal writing—quite appropriate for an in-house document and a good way to assure full readership.

Second, it contains fresh language and positive, forward thinking.

Third, it is specific, goal oriented, and well within readers' ability to perform. All organizational leaders should have about their personalities the slight flavor of a good coach, and this writer delivers.

10. Be Positive All the Time

"I'm sorry that we didn't have a chance to . . ."

"I was disappointed to learn that . . ."

"It was unfortunate that we missed each other at the conference ..."

"I wish you had given us a chance to bid on that project ..."

Openings such as these are painfully common in business writing. They put the reader on alert that what follows is not going to be pleasant. Often such an opening is as far as many readers ever get.

As a professional, you need to understand one of the most important characteristics of human nature. We like things to be positive. We don't like things that are negative.

This is not to suggest that you should be a Pollyanna, going around putting the best possible face on what are clearly negative events. Far from it. You should be forthright and upfront with readers all the time—yet understanding that the written word holds its power far longer than the spoken word.

By that same token, you can develop a reputation for positive thinking and writing that will reap many benefits in the long run.

The most successful sales representative I ever met gave me this advice:

> You can catch a cold quickly from another person. You can just as quickly catch a bad attitude. I don't stay around people who are sick. And I don't stay around people who are negative. I don't want to catch what they have! You can't sell anything to anyone with a sad face.

The reason to write in a positive voice is quite practical: It predisposes your readers to listen to your arguments.

Among trainers and teachers it's a truism that you must find good things to say about a person's work before he/she will accept criticism. There's something universally true about human nature that insists we all recognize positive things about any issue before getting to the negative.

A negative punch right out of the box is tantamount to a declaration of war. The protective shields go up and nothing gets through.

Similarly, a writer who begins negatively says, in effect, I don't care about any of the good things we can discuss. I'm going to focus on what's wrong, and you won't like it.

A negative voice puts you immediately at a disadvantage. The reader will drop out at the first possibility, and might not come back for more. Here's what Valerie Miller, a motivational speaker on the national circuit and business owner, has to say about it:

> The difference between people who have a positive attitude and people who have a negative attitude is based on our habits of word choice. Negative people develop a language full of negative words. They focus on what's wrong.
>
> Positive people think and speak in hopeful terms. They have faith in the ability to improve. They have developed a positive language.

We often use negative language simply because we don't recognize it as such.

For example, "I don't think you understood the inclusive nature of our bid versus competitors who price their services a la carte" is negative in an unthinking way. It attributes the fault to the reader.

With just a few seconds of thought, you can put a positive face on this same idea: "Please notice that our bid is all-inclusive. Our competitors may price their services differently."

Another example: Let's say you're dealing with a customer

Best Tip

Begin your letters and memos positively and professionally— even when you're delivering bad news.

who is pushing for an absurdly lower price. Your estimate is down as far as you can (or care to) go. Put your position in a positive light. Don't get into negative territory by apologizing, or regretting, or wishing. Simply reaffirm why your price is what it is. Underscore all the positive reasons for doing business with your company.

Grammar Notes

This is a book about business writing, not English grammar. Grammar is the basis of writing, however, just as strength-training is the basis of gymnastics. Several excellent grammar books are available. You'll find some of the best listed in the Bibliography. Please get a good one and keep it handy.

Grammar denotes class. Most of us like to think of ourselves as working professionals who are competent and classy. Poor grammar, however, in written or spoken communications, will damage that image. Worse, it will label the writer as less than a first-rank thinker. Clients and customers are not likely to complain about someone's grammatical lapses, but they notice.

Best Tip
Don't take chances when you are not sure a sentence is grammatically correct. Rewrite it in a way you know is right.

Even some of the best writers encounter a grammatical problem that they can't resolve on the spot. English is complicated. In these cases, you have two appropriate courses of action. Consult an English grammar handbook, or restructure the sentence to avoid the problem altogether.

Here are some common grammatical problems for you to check out. Most business writers have trouble with these; however, just a little practice will help you clear them up forever.

1. *Pronoun case.* Writers often are confused about which pronoun is correct. For example, "between you and I" should be "between you and me." "Between" is a preposition that requires an object.

2. *Verb agreement.* You often read something like "the team of employees are working on the problem." The writer mistakenly thinks "employees" is the subject that requires a plural verb. In reality, "team" is the subject and requires a singular verb.

3. *Use of semicolons and commas.* The semicolon is the most sophisticated punctuation available to us; however, there are only

specific occasions when its use is proper. If you don't know what those occasions are, don't use semicolons at all.

Commas are so common they are certain to be misused. The error I see by far the most is in a sentence like this: "She sent executive summaries to the CEO, group manager and plant managers." For some reason, most writers are determined to leave out the comma before the "and." This is a mistake. With items in a series, always use a comma before the last "and." It is always correct to use it and often incorrect or confusing to leave it out.

Another common comma problem is called the comma splice, as in, "I can't go, I have something else to do." Commas can't join two complete clauses. In this case, you need to turn that sentence into two sentences, or join them with a semicolon.

Recommendation: Spend an hour with a good grammar guide. Do not ignore grammar problems. You can learn grammar rules quickly, even self-teach, with the right materials.

The Agile Manager's Checklist

✔ Give yourself a deadline. Pressure helps you get the job done.
✔ When you're working on a group project, fill out the Planning Guide together before you write a report or make a recommendation.
✔ Spend at least a third of your time rewriting, editing, and revising.
✔ Put your main idea at the beginning, and use lots of subheads—even in short documents like letters.
✔ Use short words, short sentences, and short paragraphs.
✔ Watch your language. Use words you know, eliminate the passive voice and unnecessary words, and use a style and tone appropriate to the situation.

Chapter Five

Win with a 'You' Attitude

It was late Monday afternoon. The Agile Manager puttered around his office after getting pounded by his boss for the lackluster results in getting contract design and development work from other companies.

He finally sat down and began to compile a list of companies to call the next day to set up presentations. Suddenly, he heard a commotion in the outer office, and then a loud knock on the door. "Enter!" said the Agile Manager in a mock stentorian tone.

William burst in, looking as if he'd overdosed on espresso. "She'll see us again, she'll see us again!" The Agile Manager knew who he must be talking about, but he asked, "Who will?"

"Lynn Halsey! She wants to discuss our designs and cost estimates." He beamed.

"That's great Willie! When?"

"Wednesday at 1:15. She has to leave for the airport at 1:45, so we won't have much time. Say, do you have any good buddies in accounting?"

"Sure," said the Agile Manager. "Why?"

"Well, you know those cost estimates I said I had?"

"Yeah."

"Actually, I don't have them. But I figured it wouldn't be all that *hard to come up with solid figures. Isn't that right?"*

"Willie," groaned the Agile Manager. "Do you have component prices?"

"Not yet, but—"

"Get 'em. And have them on my desk—along with your labor estimates—by noon tomorrow. We have no time to waste."

"You bet!" William danced out of the office. The Agile Manager smiled as he heard him sprint down the hall. If we get something going with Halsey, he thought, it'll get Don off my back.

He buzzed William's desk.

"Yeah?"

"Good work, man."

This chapter will explain how to employ a "you" attitude to write successful

- Cold sales letters
- Warm prospect letters
- Brochures and other marketing collateral.

The Main Point: You must think like your prospects to have any chance of motivating them to act.

The Secondary Point: It is no longer sufficient, if in fact it ever was, to load people down with facts and thereby sell to them. You must first establish a human connection.

How to Make Sales Letters Reader-Oriented

Let's say you've just come back to the office from an industry convention with six good leads. These people have expressed at least a glimmer of interest in your product or service.

How do you follow up? In a few pages we'll get to five market-tested strategies for promoting yourself and your business in a sales letter. First, however, let's discuss what you shouldn't do, and why.

Don't begin with a review of your professional qualifications and the special advantages your business offers. Don't start like this: "I want to take a few minutes of your time . . ." or "I was hoping we could meet for a conversation about . . ."

Here's a good rule of thumb:

If you begin a letter with "I" you lose.

If you begin a letter with "You" you win.

The readers don't care about what I (the writer) want. People care about themselves and their particular challenges on the job. They don't care about me and my success. Or you and your special offer. Not just yet, at any rate.

So always start by talking about what they do care about—themselves.

Avoid the "you're lucky you met me" attitude. Here's a headline from a full-page ad that ran recently in Boston newspapers:

We've been an important part of this region's banking community since 1967.

The copy had the usual boilerplate about dedication to quality and customers, and was signed off with the bank's logo.

Now except for the chairman and president of this bank, does anyone on earth care about the information in that headline? Of course not. The bank and its advertising agency have simply failed to look at life from the customer's point of view. If they had, maybe they would have written a headline like this:

Now you can get approval on most loans within two hours.
There's a decision-making manager in a branch office near you.

OK, it won't win any awards. It simply talks to readers about a service they might find useful.

The only sure way to potential customers' hearts is to talk about their needs.

Develop the "you can win with my help" attitude. To create an effective sales letter, think of yourself as the prospect's coach.

Like most coaches, you're not on the field during this game. You're not taking the risks or getting your nose rubbed in the mud. Your prospect is.

You enjoy the safety of the sidelines. So if you talk only about your credentials as a coach, and suggest how lucky the prospect is to have you around, you may find yourself out of the stadium altogether.

However, if your attitude says, "You, Mr./Ms. prospect, are

going to win because you're good, and I'm going to help you win because I've got some ideas and services you can use to advantage," then you have a chance to coach the whole game.

Five Basic Strategies

Here are five strategies for crafting an effective sales letter based on a powerful "sympathetic coach" attitude. A sample sales letter, using these strategies, appears on page 87. If you wish, use it as a starting point for your own sales letters, until you can develop a better one based on the realities of your business.

1. Open with Your Best Shot. Too many writers save their strongest sales pitch for the end, thinking this adds dramatic punch. It doesn't. Most readers won't read to the end. Consequently, they lose your best thinking and you lose a potential customer.

Instead, come out swinging with your most compelling sales message. How do you do that? By dealing with their needs, not yours.

2. Make Your Ideas Immediately Apparent to the Reader. Does this mean you have contempt for your reader's ability to handle subtlety and nuance? Not at all. It means you have respect for your reader's time. So structure your document in such a way as to make its point obvious. In so doing, you'll also make sure that the point of the document isn't lost on *you*.

I was teaching a writing seminar to a group of business people on Boston's North Shore. As preparation, I had asked the participants to bring in a typical document on a transparency.

One woman showed the group a letter she had sent to an insurance company a few weeks before. A moving company had lost a crate of demonstration materials en route to a trade show. Her company had not only made an ineffective appearance at the convention, but also had lost business because of it. She was writing to inform the insurance company of the particulars.

"What did you want the insurance company to do?" I asked.

"Send us a check for $21,343," she said.

"Where do you say that in the letter?" I asked.

Everyone in the group scanned the document intently. Nowhere did she spell out what she wanted.

"Did you get the check yet?" I asked.

"No," she said. "Guess I'd better write another letter."

I recommended she begin the new letter with this line: Action requested.

The best way to make your content obvious is with subheads.

3. Talk Person to Person, Not Human Resource to Human Resource. You have a personality; use it to advantage. People like to talk to people. Be direct, personable, forthright, unpretentious. Choose words as you write the same way you would choose them if you were speaking to the person by phone or face to face.

The key, I believe, is to tell the truth in a compelling way. The quality of your ideas, simply expressed—not the size of your vocabulary—will impress prospects.

4. Be Politely Aggressive. Go ahead. Ask for the order loud and clear. Few people ever prosper in sales without asking the customer to buy. There's nothing to be shy about.

Ask for the sale, however, in the context of meeting the prospect's needs: "I am confident of asking for your business because I am among the few vendors who can precisely meet your needs at a good price."

Getting someone to devote a few moments of attention to your letter is a major breakthrough. Don't blow it by being shy or unclear. Ask for the business, and do it the way a sympathetic coach would do it—with firmness and a little sense of humor.

5. Now Demonstrate Your Qualifications. At last, we're finally at the point where you can talk about yourself! If the prospects like what you're saying so far, they're now looking for any assurance that you can handle the job. So give it to them in a suitably forthright, non-bragging tone. Never start with credentials; end with them.

A quick anecdote of some recent success might go well here. It's also a good time to demonstrate familiarity with the prospect's industry or with his/her particular challenges. Go for it, but still maintain that "you" attitude that got you this far.

An Example

Here's an example to tie all these ideas together for you.

Mr. James Prospect
Metro Industries
123 Main Street
Middletown, USA

Dear Mr. Prospect:

You asked me to get back to you with a few ideas when we spoke at last week's Tech-World Show, and I'm happy to respond.

How to counter expanding foreign competition

Your company can beat domestic competition and even some foreign manufacturers' prices. But growing competition from countries where labor is much cheaper is a big threat.

The way I see it, you have three options:
1. Lower your prices and take significant cuts in profits
2. Expand into cheap-labor countries yourself
3. Strengthen your reputation for unusually high quality at bargain prices.

Proposal for action

Clearly, there is no simple answer to this challenge. Most major U.S. firms face similar crises. (Cold comfort, I know.) But there are several positive steps you can take.

Within these options there is a range of possibilities, such as getting a better idea of competitors' plans, researching the image your products now hold in the marketplace, and crafting a detailed five-year plan. Even in our brief conversation, I sensed you could use some outside expert help in these areas.

I propose a qualitative competitive research instrument. I can offer two practical suggestions about keeping costs well within the budget figures we discussed.

How I can be of most help to you

My field is foreign expansion. I can put together a plan for you similar to the one I did for Port Enterprises in New York. It ended up saving them $1.7 million over three years. I've enclosed (with their permission) a copy of the initial questionnaire I created for them, along with top-line results.

I'll call you in five days

Once you've had a chance to review this material, I'll call on the twenty-fifth to see if you wish to move forward. I will be able to fax you a timeline at that point so you can see how quickly we can gather this information. Please call me sooner if you wish.

I know my experience can benefit your organization in this critical area. It was a pleasure to meet you. Thanks for letting me share some ideas.

Sincerely yours,

Julie Winner

P.S. The president of Port Enterprises, Jack Webbly, said he would be glad to give you a recommendation for us over the phone. He's at 555-8787.

How to Edit the Writing of Others

The "you" attitude is a winning strategy for dealing with others. It works with every level of people of interest to your organization: suspects, prospects, customers, and advocates. It works with people up and down your own organization as well.

It's particularly effective with people who write documents directly for your approval.

Tread Carefully When Evaluating

You should be aware that receiving improper or destructive criticism of one's writing is among the most painful of life's experiences.

It ranks with being fired for an emotional low point. Supervisors tend to dash off comments on the writing of their direct reports with little thought for the impact those comments might have.

Writing is revealing the quality of your thinking, of your ideas. Negative, thoughtless criticism undercuts confidence and leaves long-lasting scars. It says the writer does not measure up.

In one of my workshops, most of the participants worked for the same supervisor. To an individual, they showed me documents they had prepared for this person's approval. There were giant red *X*s over whole paragraphs, even whole pages. Sometimes the supervisor would write "NO" or "STUPID THINKING" in red block letters across a page.

This was the worst case of insensitive critiquing I had ever seen. The people who worked for this supervisor felt helpless and of little worth. Sadly, however, much of the critiquing by supervisors is potentially damaging. Even where there is no intent to inflict emotional hurt, the possibility remains that people will be frustrated by unhelpful criticism.

Often supervisors are commenting on issues they know little or nothing about. They:

- Take out commas that are properly placed, and add commas incorrectly
- Add dozens of words to an already incomprehensible sentence
- Insert a colon where a semicolon is called for
- Make other mistakes in grammar and word choice.

Supervisors comment rarely on issues that they should be qualified for, like the dynamic arrangement of the document or strategic placement of the main idea. They also seldom comment on:

- The quality of the visual presentation
- The use of subheads and graphs
- The value of the attachments
- The recommendations/conclusions
- The proper/improper placement of background.

Ensure a Smooth Critiquing Process in Three Steps

If you supervise the writing of others, or if someone directly supervises your writing, I suggest you call a meeting of everyone involved and agree on the following criteria.

1. Fill out the Planning Guide together. Nothing promotes buy-in or the smoothest possible flow of a writing project better than mutual agreement on the central issues contained in the Planning Guide (see page 19).

This is where all parties concerned should hammer out the basics of the document—not in a polished draft. Doing it up front saves time, money, effort, and immeasurable frustration up and down the line.

Best Tip

Hammer out the basics of a document with employees in the early stages—never when they hand in a polished piece.

Face to face working out of the issues is always best. Why? I don't know. I've done it all kinds of ways, from personal meetings to conference calls to e-mail piled upon e-mail. Face to face works.

There's something about seeing other people's expressions, gauging their interest level and the political ramifications, that happens only in person.

Maybe it's the same principle that applies to juries in a courtroom. They need to see the faces of witnesses. Hearing voices only or watching via remote TV simply won't do.

2. Ask to see an extensive outline of the idea arrangement before writing begins. Here, too, the Planning Guide is valuable. Can your main point go at the top? If so, agree on one of the outlines explained on pages 42 to 55 that features your main point or recommendations at the top, and go from there.

A good editor will suggest an idea arrangement early in the writing process.

3. Suggest improvements of a working draft based on agreed-upon criteria. You might want to create your own criteria as a team based on the realities of your workplace. Until you develop such a document, please consider using the following checklist.

WORKING DRAFT REVIEW

✔ indicates Yes. **X** indicates No.

____ Overall content reflects Planning Guide
____ Performed brainstorming, mindmapping, questioning, or other idea-generating technique
____ Research complete
____ Main point properly placed
____ Ideas arranged in an effective structure
____ Generous use of verb-driven subheads
____ "You" attitude throughout
____ Lean, concise prose
____ Active voice
____ 50% professional/50% personable style
____ Positive viewpoint

You should add to or take away from this list as you please. If possible, everyone involved should agree on the changes. If you are the supervisor, put a ✔ or **X** on each line, staple this sheet to the document, and hand back to the writer. Make as many comments on the document itself as you wish. Make those comments in a cool color ink such as green or blue. (Red is a hot, threatening color.) Put your comments in constructive terms. Some examples:

"Please check handbook for semicolon use"

"Consider placing this paragraph farther back"

"Can you streamline this paragraph even more?"

"Sentence is 38 words. Can you break up or streamline?"

"You delay mentioning your main idea until sentence #5. Can you get to it immediately?"

Remember to write as many comments praising the work as criticizing it.

The Main Point

If you are getting paid for any of the time you spend writing, then you are a professional writer. Know your tools like any professional, and learn to use them well.

Technology, the global marketplace, increased competition—these and many other contemporary realities have pushed us all into a new era of business writing. The old, excessively formal style of writing has gone into the museum, along with the buggy whip and long-play record album.

As always happens when the times force us into new arenas, the search for solutions to new challenges is far more exciting than maintaining the status quo ever could be.

For most of us, success depends at least partially on writing effective documents. The new era of writing is a challenge well met as long as your documents, like this book, begin and end with "You."

The Agile Manager's Checklist

✔ Remember: Begin with "I" and you lose. Begin with "you" and you win.

✔ Don't hide the point of your document. Make it loud and clear.

✔ Ask for the order or whatever it is you want. Don't be shy. If you've done your work properly, you stand ready to deliver benefits.

✔ Be careful in editing the writing of others. Thoughtless criticism leaves scars.

✔ Create something like the Working Draft Review. It'll save you lots of time and headaches.

Index

*B*ibliography

These books are essential writer's tools. Keep them handy for reference, inspiration, and support.

The Business Writer's Handbook
Brusaw, Alred, and Oliu
St. Martin's Press

The Chicago Manual of Style
University of Chicago Press

The Elements of Style
Strunk & White
MacMillan Company

The New International Dictionary of Quotations
Rawson & Miner
New American Library

The New York Times Manual of Style and Usage
Jordan
New York Times Book Company

Saying What You Mean
Robert Claiborne
W.W. Norton & Co.

Vest-Pocket Guide to Business Writing
Deborah Dumaine
Prentice Hall

Write to the Top: Writing for Corporate Success
Deborah Dumaine
Random House